Some Paths

to

SUDDEN WEALTH

$

by

H. Glenn Carson

SOME PATHS TO SUDDEN WEALTH

H. Glenn Carson

Printed by
CARSON ENTERPRISES
Drawer 71, Deming, New Mexico 88031

ISBN 0-941620-44-1

TABLE OF CONTENTS

INTRODUCTION

I hope you will enjoy these brief journeys along some rather untraveled paths taken by a few individuals. For the few, these paths led to sudden wealth. These accounts are not made here to serve as easily followed guidelines. This is no attempt to give the quick fix, the instant gratification, the easy answers so many seem to want these days. There will be those who want more details from these deliberately anonymous people. I can sympathize with those feelings, but these stories would not be shared here or elsewhere if the precious privacy of these people was not respected. These brief tales are not meant to be a blueprint for others to follow to their own greater wealth. If anything more than interesting glimpses of others' successes, they perhaps offer encouragement to those who'd also like to find some unique path towards sudden wealth.

Nor is there any attempt to define wealth or place a value upon it. Sudden wealth can be marvelously beneficial or totally ruinous. That largely depends upon the individual who gains it. Many of us find such accounts interesting. What each of us would do in a similar case is usually unrecognized until sudden wealth arrives.

Believe or disbelieve, it is remarkable that a few people discover unusual routes to success and have the persistence to follow such paths. It is easier to pass along such stories than it is for the travelers along such paths to follow them. Perhaps the time is right, for a few, maybe there are lucky friendships or acquaintances, there may be a certain vision or foresight. Who can really say? It gives many of us, however, a happy glow just to witness the reaching of great success by one who struggled hard to achieve it.

Would you care to find such a path for yourself? The route is no doubt there somewhere within you, if that is what you truly wish, already partly mapped out, requiring only further goals and great ambition. Following others' paths does not seem to work well. Seek and follow your own path! By all means, use these and other such tales to give you ideas and inspiration. Enjoy the victories of others. Know, however, the goals you set yourself, the paths you choose to follow, that is what will bring you the greatest fulfillment.

SUDDEN WEALTH FOR THE COMMON MAN

This book is about sudden wealth. Not just any sudden wealth, mind you, but wealth gained by the so-called common man. Wealth gained by rather ordinary people coming up with unique ideas and visions and persistently making those dreams come true.

No effort will be made here to somehow define what makes up a "common man". One thing is for sure, wealth or a lack of it is the poorest sort of measurement for the quality of individuals. Most of us are common enough, most of us have the ability to be more than we are.

Here the term, "common man", is used to set aside that rare person who somehow from within finds a path to sudden wealth. There is nothing very common about that unique sort of individual, and their stories are fascinating.

The usual routes to success will not be studied here. Yes, quite ordinary folks choose to become doctors, lawyers, morticians, high tech salespeople, dentists, bureaucrats or enter into other fields where a good possibility of wealth exists. Less well established paths to wealth are explored here, perhaps the sorts of paths only the so-called common man might risk taking. Such paths are not well marked. No equivalent of medical school, no formal bar exam, nothing of that sort. There are not even too many books or articles on the subject to alert or encourage would-be seekers of different routes to success.

Truthfully, the heroes of these pages are not commonplace. They are extraordinary individuals, who merit much praise. They come from nowhere. They start with little or nothing. They recognize the faintest of paths toward an ill-defined goal, and gain their education on a difficult journey along that poorly marked path.

Along with all that, the wealth they seek often eludes them for a very long time. We can honestly talk about sudden wealth, because for some persistent dreamers and doers wealth does arrive suddenly and splendidly where there was none before. Sudden wealth, more than they had ever really hoped for, obtained as a result of their own efforts.

Uncommon, these dreamers and doers, not at all common!

FIRST HAND WEALTH FROM SECOND HAND JUNK

So many things are thrown away in this country! Mountains of refuse fill up the dumps to overflowing. Lifetime accumulations of odds and ends sometimes trickle, sometimes pour into the flea markets, junk stores, pawnshops, yard sales, and other such places. Estate auctions, bankruptcy auctions, moving sales, and heirs cleaning out estates offer endless values.

Much of this mass of material is not of huge value, but most of it has some value. Not nearly enough of that is salvaged. Some of it, this and that, here and there, is extremely valuable.

A good many years back, Ralph Baker began to realize that a real opportunity to make some money existed in the pawn shops, antique stores, second hand and junk stores, yard and garage sales, and all sorts of auctions. Yes, even from the ever expanding dumps. No, Ralph Baker is not the man's real name.

Ralph had tried to work for a couple of big corporations. He had tried some selling, but had only mild success. He had not gone to college, but he was a voracious reader. No youngster anymore, Ralph Baker began to explore the potential of finding gems in junk.

He did not find his niche easily or quickly, but he eventually found it. His story merely shows that persistence, not magic, makes things happen.

There was plenty of furniture in auctions and yard sales. Some buying and selling convinced him that dealing in furniture meant some heavy lifting, almost endless cleaning, stripping, and refinishing, and the need for a big truck and plenty of storage and work area. Neither liking the refinishing work nor having a big truck or storage area, Ralph slowly began concentrating his efforts on smaller items.

Once in a while opportunity doesn't knock, it nearly beats your door down. If a person doesn't seize that opportunity, it rushes on by. One such event is what actually set Ralph Baker onto his personal path to sudden wealth.

In a small Indiana town he by happenstance met a frantic fellow of about sixty years of age. The man was a nephew who had recently inherited his aunt's estate. He had a buyer for his aunt's large old house, but the place was absolutely full of junk from the attic to the basement. Every closet, every room, every nook and cranny was jam packed full of furniture, cartons, boxes, sacks and containers of who knew what. The garage and two sheds at the back of the lot were filled with dusty, cobwebbed piles, hardly room to open the door.

The nephew was an excitable sort of person, and not in too good health. He was from out of state and did not want to stay there any longer than he had to. He was frantic, because of the pending sale of the property. He wanted to have an estate sale, but the prospective buyer wanted to take possession of the property within a short time. The contents of the property obviously were not as important to him as was the sale of the property.

"What do you want for all of the stuff, if I'd clean this mess up for you?" Ralph asked the frantic heir, after talking with him for a time .

"It's worth thousands!" said the man, "My aunt had some very good things."

"That may be," Ralph replied, "but it is a big mess. You sound like you are in a hurry. Would you take a thousand dollars?"

The other man hesitated. He fidgeted and thought for a considerable time. "I guess I would, but only if you can get it cleaned out of here in three days."

"You have a deal," said Ralph. "I will get on it within the hour."

Ralph got hold of the biggest rental moving truck in town. He rounded up two husky men to help him. Before the end of the second day he had to rent another truck, but before the end of the third day he had everything out of the house, the garage, and the sheds. He paid off the now relieved heir. He had his helpers follow him with the second truckload to a nearby, somewhat larger town. He rented a large storage shed there and assisted his helpers in unloading both trucks into it. They then returned the trucks to the rental agency, he paid off the men. He returned in his car to the other town, and rented a motel room nearby the storage shed.

It took Ralph the better part of three weeks to sort through his purchase. The heir had been right, his aunt had some very good things. She also had accumulated all sorts of absolute trash.

There was considerable furniture, far more than any normal family would need to furnish their home. Ralph had recently given up any effort to work with furniture, but he knew several people who did. The fourth man he called was close enough to be willing to come see what Ralph was talking about.

"What do want for all of it?" his acquaintance asked.

"You mean all the furniture?"

"Yeah."

"It ought to be worth three thousand or more, certainly not less than twenty seven, twenty eight hundred."

"You still believe in the tooth fairy, I see. I wouldn't give you more than seventeen, eighteen hundred for the lot."

There was some more haggling, but Ralph Baker finally took $2,000. His acquaintance brought a truck, a couple of men to help him, and drove away with all the furniture. The volume of Mr. Baker's purchase was less than half of what it had been.

By the time he sold the furniture, Ralph had fairly well sorted everything. He concentrated like things together. For some categories a small box was enough. He'd not let any of the paintings the old lady had go with the furniture, and there were several dozen. There were several boxes of tools. There were boxes of dishes and cookware. There were several boxes of carefully wrapped china and crystal. There was sterling silver. Linens, lace, blankets, comforters, quilts and a considerable amount of clothing was packed into a large pile of boxes. Much of it was of fine quality, and much of it must have been packed away in the old lady's girlhood or before. There was men's, women's, boys', girls', and babies' clothing.

From here and there through all of it he had taken small boxes, jars, and packages of old coins, old currency, and no small amount of jewelry. There were several small sheaves of currency, each carefully and well wrapped. There were six diamond rings, two of which had substantial diamonds. There were several sets of pearl necklaces. There were numerous other rings, brooches, necklaces and pins.

Ralph almost filled five boxes with dolls and doll dresses, and he had a dozen sacks or boxes of various toys. Some of them were very old.

There were boxes and stacks of items any house would have. This lot was enough to have served three or four normal houses. Yard tools, kitchen ware, pillows, crocks, vases, a nice old world globe, fans, thermos jugs. All sorts of things people would have accumulated from obviously before the turn of the century.

Much of it was actual trash. That

was, in fact, the biggest pile of all when Ralph Baker at last decided he had sorted well enough.

The old lady had a large number of quality books, most in excellent shape. Ralph put a few he wanted aside, then called five or six book dealers. None of them wanted to come see them, said it was too far. One, however, was on the route to Columbus, Ohio, where Ralph wanted to soon go.

When he finally went by on his way to Columbus, Ralph sold the books to that dealer for $270. Ralph knew the man would probably get ten times that amount for them, or more, but he didn't care. It would take a good deal of time, and Ralph was not interested in selling a book at a time.

Before he left, Ralph sold much of the incidental stuff to a local junkstore dealer for a fifty dollar bill, provided the man would haul away all the trash. He was there when the man loaded it up, making sure nothing else went at that time.

The month's rent was not up on the storage shed when Ralph brought around a much smaller rental truck than the one he'd used before. He was not concerned about that, he wanted to drive to Columbus. He knew a jewelry dealer there.

He sold the jewelry for not quite four thousand dollars. He held back the best diamond ring and the nicest set of pearls. Remember, this was a good many years ago.

He set aside all the ordinary currency. $1,623. That went into his billfold. An additional $217 face was made up of obviously very old bills. There was $518.43 in coinage. $52.76 of that was in recent coinage, Ralph knew that much of the rest had at least some numismatic value.

He sold several vases and some other items to an antique dealer in Columbus for just over $300. He held back three of the paintings, thinking they could be valuable, sold all the others to three different dealers. That added up to not quite $700. The $217 face in old bills he sold to a coin shop owner for $415.

He knew that he was leaving plenty of room for the buyers to make large mark ups. The fact was, his smaller truck was beginning to empty out. He decided in a few more days to take the truck back to the town where he'd rented the storage shed. He picked up his car, crammed what was left in the rental truck into the car, and turned in the rental truck.

A few of the things Ralph Baker bought from that frantic heir he still has. He sold the rest of it over a period of several years. He received more from a good many single items than he did from everything he sold in the first two months. One of the three paintings brought him almost ten times the results of those first two month's work. The second painting he sold for $900. The third he finally sold for a ten dollar bill, to a woman who bought it because she wanted the frame.

Ralph later learned that the fellow who bought all the furniture netted almost ten thousand dollars from it. He also let it slip that he'd recovered some currency from a writing desk. He would only smile when Ralph asked him how much. Ralph had no regrets or complaints. Over the years he sold other lots of furniture to that same man.

Ralph Baker at first often went to estate sales. Sometimes he did well. Often he bought nothing at all. He did not enjoy the high pressure, and it was often too easy to be rushed into making mistakes. Some of his friends and acquaintances did extremely well in that kind of environment, but Ralph began to turn his attention elsewhere.

He did not sell at the flea markets.

He sold to flea marketers, but he wanted to spend more time out hunting.

He began to do very well in small junk shops in smaller towns, and in little antique shops tucked out of the way. He especially liked to be early at garage and yard sales. More and more he looked for odds and ends that were not common to whatever part of the country he was in. For instance he found some Pacific Northwest Indian carvings down in Georgia. The operator had no idea of where they had come from or their value. In Idaho he once found a small box of scrimshaw, probably from some early Massachusetts port. The owner of the junkstore there was delighted to get twenty five dollars for the box. He found sixteen various Arizona Territory trade tokens resting in a cup in a Wisconsin Antique Boutique. The lady there wanted a quarter each, but he could have them for a dime each if he'd take them all. Yes, one of them was from Fort Bowie.

Over the years Ralph Baker made even better deals than that first big one. He never made one that was so completely rewarding. One would have to say that frantic heir showed Ralph Baker the gateway to his very own path to sudden wealth.

GEORGE BRONTE'S POCKET GOLD

Few people would ever think, looking at him, that George Bronte found a reliable path to sudden wealth many years ago. Few enough ever see much of George, as far as that goes, because he is usually off in out of the way places doing what he knows so well how to do. Those who meet him see a short, wiry man never dressed in anything fancier than some old jeans, work boots, a nondescript shirt, and an old Stetson well past its prime. He's always clean, but his clothes most often have some dirt on them from his work.

Early on George Bronte became fascinated with gold recovery. The results were never good enough to allow him to stop doing other work. Panning proved to be an excellent way to prospect, but it was too hard and too slow to make much money. Rockers worked well for George, but most placer sites were not rich enough or extensive enough to give him even a meager living. Various sluices or dredges were little better. Scuba diving was for George something to be left entirely to others.

He kept at it, going into good gold country whenever he'd saved up enough money to take off work for a time. George enjoyed working by himself, being out there alone doing what he most wanted to do. He just could not make a living at it. He would every time soon have to go back to one job or another.

George ran into an old pocket hunter named Caleb Morton in California's Mother Lode country after several years of his gold hunting efforts. Caleb had watched George Bronte for some long time, and was impressed by his desire and persistence. So-called pocket hunters never were too common, and Caleb was one of the last of the old time pocket hunters. Caleb introduced himself, and then told and showed George how to recover pocket gold. In a short time the old man turned around the course of George Bronte's life.

Bronte quickly learned that recovering pocket gold is far different than placering. Both require careful prospecting for the best possible working sites. There are huge differences beyond that similarity.

Placer gold is characteristically rounded, smoothed by stream action. It is surrounded by sand, gravel, and boulders, either in current stream beds or in ancient ones. Pocket gold. is much different. It has characteristically rough, sharp planes and surfaces, the edges are not smooth. It often is well concealed by a surface patina of rusty magnesium and iron oxides. Flakes and bits often look more like black sand than they do gold.

Placer gold is that which has been eroded from its original vein structure, dragged by gravity downhill into streams, and pounded and rounded by water action and ongoing abrasion of various surrounding particles.

Pocket gold is also from its original vein structure, shed as a quartz vein or other source is rotted and weathered, eaten by the corrosive reactions of oxygen and other natural forces. The far more resistant gold simply drops out of its matrix, is dragged down along its vein structure by gravity and various earth movements over incredibly long periods of time. If the gold reaches the surface, it washes downhill and becomes placer gold. If it works its way down along the vein structure without reaching the surface as the vein decomposes, it joins an ever enlarging pocket at a point where the vein constricts and pinches out.

Small tremors, large, vicious earthquakes, any tiny movement of the earth is enough force to gradually move the bits and pieces of gold down along the disintigrating vein structure. At the point where a vein structure actually or nearly pinches out there is no longer any way the gold can go deeper. At that point a pocket of gold is deposited. The size of the deposit is dependent upon the size of the original vein, its gold content, and how deep it is to the point where the vein pinches out.

These deposits are almost always of a rusty hue. Dull orange. Ochre is perhaps the best description of such material. That is not surprising, for gold is closely associated with iron. Oxides often stain the individual particles, blackening them. The entire mass is of brownish hues. Ochre, with a snuff-like appearance, rusty, reddish brown, not looking at all like what most people think gold should look like.

Old Caleb Morton right up front made it clear to George that pocket hunting was not for anyone afraid of work, not observant, or unable to do some good thinking. Placering is far easier in most respects. That was why many people placered, why so few ever did much pocket hunting even if they knew about it.

Hard work and clear thinking of course leaves a great majority of people out of doing something as demanding as hunting for pocket gold.

Just as one would prospect for placer gold, Caleb showed George how to prospect his way up a likely looking stream. Country with a great deal of broken and weathered quartz was considered the best place to start by the old-time pocket hunters. One would pan a sample every hundred yards or so as he worked his way upstream. Continue upstream as long as the pan continued to show color. At whatever point there were no more colors, the search was moved back to the last place to show color. The source of those colors was uphill from there, on one side of the creek or the other.

It was several years after this beginning that George Bronte realized that there could be more than once decomposed vein structure along that hillside. That is especially true if colors are found in the stream over a long distance, or the amount of colors vary over various distances.

The challenge is then to find the source. As pocket gold is almost always well below the surface, and usually shows no surface indications, the source can only be located by further prospecting.

The most practical method of doing such prospecting is crude, simple, but effective. A series of sample holes, about six inches to a foot in depth, is dug in a line parallel to the stream bed, upstream and downstream from that stopping place. Samples are taken from the material from those holes. Each hole must be staked and numbered. Each sample is carefully panned for colors. If one hillside produces no colors, the hillside on the other side of the stream is sampled.

When particles of gold are found, another shorter row of test holes is dug parallel to the stream about a hundred feet farther up the hillside. There is no need to dig above where no colors are found, nor to make the row of holes wider along the hill than is necessary. George knows the gold is coming from some yet unseen decayed vein somewhere above him on the hillside. The colors are the primary path to finding that spot. Every sample must be carefully panned for colors. Step by step, in a pyramid or triangular fashion, the shorter and shorter rows of test holes are dug up the hillside until a point is reached where there were no more colors.

If one diagrams this, either upon paper or within one's mind, the ever shorter rows of test holes, form something of an arrow. This "arrow" points directly to the site of the yet unseen decayed gold-bearing vein.

"It's dull work, but it has to be done," Caleb often told him. "If you don't keep track of where each sample comes from, if you don't pan each sample carefully and keep notes, you don't have a chance of finding where to dig. If you do it right, it leads you right to where you can find the vein."

That final spot, where no more colors show up in the pan, should be well marked. The gold source is somewhat downhill from there. Additional probing and digging usually pinpoints the exact location of the old vein structure. More bits of gold and disintegrated quartz are the giveaway clues to the vein structure.

That point is where the real work begins. "This is what separates the men from the boys," Caleb would say. "This is why there never have been too many pocket hunters. It's damned hard work!" A vertical, slanted, or horizontal digging large enough to work in is started into the hillside. Timbering has to be done if the surrounding material is loose. The vein structure, well-rotted, usually takes no more than pick and shovel work. As work progresses, a windlass or some other means of getting out the debris has to be set up.

As work continues, bits and pieces of quartz show the direction of the old vein. Samples are often taken and carefully panned, more of them as the hole deepens. As one nears the pocket the material becomes richer. More and more dull brown colors show up. About five to ten feet from the pocket, sharp, rough bits and pieces of gold are often encountered. Almost all of the material is worth panning or sluicing. Black, brown, ugly, the material does not look like gold. Even so, it acts like gold, hangs heavy in the pan, and it IS gold.

Old timers used a mixture of vinegar, oxalic acid, and salt to remove the discoloration. Bronte discovered that Clorox worked as well or better.

Old man Morton passed on to George a belief he shared with a few other old time pocket hunters. They observed that often these pockets of ochre gold on old veins came in threes. There was a top, middle, and lower pocket on the same vein. The first pocket was usually twenty feet or so below the surface. It was the smallest of the three deposits upon the vein. Although the vein actually or almost pinched out, it did not end completely. The constriction was enough to trap considerable gold, forming that first, upper pocket. If more work was done, a second pocket could usually be found down at about the forty or forty-five foot level. Almost always, that second pocket was two, three, five times larger than the first one. Another twenty feet, often thirty feet or so, a third pocket often existed. There usually was more distance between the second and third pockets than there was between the first and second. If it was there, the pocket was five to ten or more times larger than the second one.

It is work aplenty to reach the first pocket. Most of the old time pocket hunters either did not realize the possibility of lower pockets along the vein, or did not want to do that much work. Few of the old pocket hunters ever took out more than the first pocket.

There were few enough of the old pocket hunters. There are even fewer new pocket hunters and the new ones seldom are willing to work as hard as the old timers did. That was why Caleb was willing, even desirous of passing along his knowledge to Bronte.

George listened well to the old man. He rather quickly located his first decayed vein, just the way Caleb told him he'd have to do it. He dug down, following the traces of quartz and rusty colored materials, carefully shoring up the sides of his hole to keep his working area safe. He located and removed about a cubic foot of ochre material at less than twenty feet almost straight down into the hillside. Gold was still only $35 in those days, and the pocket netted him just over $300. Not bad in those hard days! Similar pockets these days are worth at least twenty times as much in our inflated currency, or about $6,000.

George Bronte never ceases to be amazed that $300 back then would buy just about the same as $6,000 will buy today.

George Bronte did not rest on his laurels. Within the first year after that first recovery, he cleaned out almost ten other pockets. The next two or three after the first one were of about the same value. He then went back to the site of the first recovery, and dug deeper along the old vein. He was even more careful with his timbering and shoring. Sure enough, there was almost five times as much gold in a second pocket. It was a tall, almost oval deposit starting twenty-six feet lower than the first, nearly five feet up and down the vein. George was paid almost $1,500 net for the rusty looking material. It was enough sudden wealth in those days to put George Bronte forever solidly on his feet. He never again had to go back to a fill-in job .

Several times now, Bronte has recovered three pockets going down the same old vein. Never more, although he dug on down in two places, just to be sure. The old timers had a reason for believing there was a limit of three deposits on one vein. Oxidation seldom if ever goes deeper than seventy or eighty feet, and without oxidation the vein does not disintegrate. No disintigration, no pocket gold.

One of George's most recent efforts was going back to that original site to dig down and attempt to recover a possible third pocket. With somewhat over twenty-five additional feet of digging, he encountered a large pocket that was at least eight times larger than the second one he'd removed from that same vein. Gold at that time was selling at almost $400 per ounce. He received just over a quarter of a million dollars for less than the three months work it took him to do the job.

It was not the only project for him that year. Although it was his best project that year, it was not best by all that much. One project after that, and two before then have been even better.

He learned to look over all old hillside diggings in prime gold country. If there were great amounts of quartz scattered throughout a fairly small pile, he figured it could well be where an old timer went after a first pocket. Bigger waste piles meant that they probably went deeper. If panning produced even a few brown, black, heavy, sharp particles, he considered digging deeper on the vein. That conclusion worked well for George over the years.

The second or third pocket was always lower, but at times was not straight down. He just followed the vein, no matter how it twisted, after he picked it up below where it had pinched off to form the first pocket. Bits and pieces of rotten quartz always showed him the way.

George Bronte has done most of his pocket hunting throughout the Mother Lode Country of California. He did spend most of one summer on a good spot in Idaho, profitably enough. He also tried a spot one winter not too far from Yuma, Arizona. He simply was familiar with California, and seldom saw much reason to go elsewhere. George would be the first to say that wherever good placer gold is found there is also a good possibility of there being good pocket gold in that same area. Bronte thinks it would be foolish to not stay in one good area once a person becomes familiar and comfortable with it. Even where pocket hunting has been extensively done, with most of the surface pockets cleaned out, there still very likely remain the deeper, richer pockets. That is because they are harder to find. There are fewer surface traces, and there is so much hard work necessary to reach them.

George is slowing down. He is not worried about giving away "secrets". Not everyone wants to work or think hard enough to do what he has done. He long ago found his path to sudden wealth, and feels that anyone willing to work as hard and thoughtfully as he has done should have the chance to fare as well. The old timers felt that for every pocket they recovered they left a hundred. Bronte feels that they were most conservative in that belief. They seldom went after the second or third pockets, even though such pockets were increasingly richer.

George Bronte has truly found pockets full of sudden wealth!

AVOIDING NEGATIVE PEOPLE AND SITUATIONS

The central figures in this book are positive people. Self confident, goal oriented, realistically optimistic, they set their sights high and were persistent in their efforts. Every one of them somehow sensed or learned how to avoid negative people and situations as much as possible.

There are always more than enough dour souls to tell those who would seek new paths they might as well not even try. Discouragement is a common fare, a sour slop, foul enough to choke the strongest throat. Encouragement, a rare and tasty treat fit to feed one's very soul, is set too seldom before us. Cruel jibes and taunts are hurled from those afraid to try anything new. Harsh, negative input is seemingly available from every direction. One who would seek a path to possible wealth must avoid as much of that destructive input as possible.

If anyone near you is constantly negative, that person should be avoided. If situations hold one back, and conditions are detrimental to advancement, one should try to remove or insulate themselves from those situations and conditions. Yes, that is often difficult to do, but it necessary if a new path is to be successfully followed. Parents, relation, friends, neighborhoods, habits, institutions, and all sorts of things often are a part of a general black cloud of negativism. They must be avoided. If any such force has too strong a hold, it must be removed as surely as if it were a cancerous growth. One cannot follow the narrow paths to any great goal carrying a load of destructive negativism.

Flee it. Find your path. Go forward upon it. Do not let negative people and situations hold you back.

OBIE TAYLOR'S FOOD WAGON

Somewhere along through the years Obie Taylor realized that people are in the habbit of eating. They eat today, and for some reason they want to eat tomorrow. He also realized that for each person to consume filet mignon, caviar, and expensive champagne, there are hundreds or even thousands who only have hot dogs or hamburgers, washed down by maybe coffee or Coke.

Not having the couple of hundred thousand dollars it takes anymore to set up a mediocre cafe, let alone the half million or more required these days to establish a nice restaurant, Obie decided to cater to simple, everyday tastes.

Obie Taylor was a putterer. He did just about anything, and did it well. He just did not like to be pushed. No job was too big if he could only tackle it at his own pace. Since a cafe was beyond his ability, and a restaurant was not even in his dreams, Obie bought himself a fourteen foot travel trailer. He knew that he could turn it into a food wagon.

It did not cost him much, because the trailer had been used pretty hard. Dings, dents, and scratches in everything made the former owner willing to sell for a few hundred dollars. That was fine by Obie. He didn't buy it to live in the beat up old thing, he wanted to make a food wagon of it. The basic structure was sound, the roof didn't leak, and it had good tires.

It took Obie only a few days to rip out the trailer's insides. He sold most of furnishings and materials to a local flea marketer for a few dollars, with the condition he also would take away all the trash.

There Obie sat, with an old, cleaned out trailer. He proceeded to clean it from one end to the other, repair any and all dings and scratches, and then gave it a good base coat of paint.

While working on the trailer, Obie bought a popcorn maker from another vendor. That man was moving elsewhere, and gave Obie a real bargain.

Over the next few weeks Obie cranked up the popcorn maker, selling a sackful now and then as he worked. He had a space just past the junction of two streets, and it didn't take long for the word to spread. From one batch early in the morning Obie soon was having to pop up two or three more batches each day.

That slowed his work on the trailer at times, but Obie never got worried or in a hurry. A few handsful of coins each day began to add up to a good many dollars, and every day there was plenty enough done to the trailer.

He figured out exactly where he wanted his sinks, counters, and storage areas. He knew that the state and county health departments demanded three sinks in a food wagon, so he allowed for that. There would have to be a fan and vent over the grill area. Room for a small freezer and a refrigerator must be allowed. Corners had to be rounded.

Slowly, perhaps, but day by day the counters went up, doors were hung on storage areas, and this or that was accomplished. The electrical work seemed to take forever, but Obie got some good help when he could not get done himself what he wanted to do. The friend, who owed him several favors, got him past that quandry in a hurry.

The popcorn machine was put atop the new counter, and enough was selling to take care of daily expenses. Obie had the chance to buy a cotton candy machine, so he bought it. That went back into a corner until where he wanted to put it was finished.

By this time Obie had begun to paint a few signs. He was a master sign painter, and without a doubt, he could have made a good living concentrating on that skill alone. He just did not want to.

A jolly, smiling clown soon brightened up the back of the trailer. That was like a beacon, there where those roads came together, and Obie by then was popping at least four batches a day as well as spinning several dozen cotton candy cones.

Several awnings, new, bigger windows, a hinged platform where orders could be taken and food delivered, window screens, and all sorts of additional improvements later, Obie Taylor's food wagon was at last taking shape.

The real magic, and the result seemed like magic if one could have seen the original trailer, was in Obie's plodding persistence and careful planning. He knew what the health departments wanted. He knew of and by then had the permits the city required. He had his sales tax number, for he'd been buying and selling things for years. In short, what Obie needed, he found out how to get.

He purchased a potato slicer that cut a single long strip from one potato. Curly fries were fairly new. They were easy to cook, and people seemed to like them even better than regular fries.

Obie decided to concentrate on hot dogs, and began to set up what he needed. He would make hamburgers, eventually, but not yet.

Some more signs went up. Obie painted a rotund fellow wearing a crown, hot dog in one hand, pointing with the other hand to the food wagon. The figure wore a sign: HOT DOG KING! Yummy hot dogs, only 79 cents. EAT LIKE A KING CHEAP!

Before he knew it, Obie had more

business than he really wanted. Hot dogs and curly fries, soft drinks, simple fare but people liked his product. He also was selling more popcorn.

Obie did not want to hire extra help. He'd thought of developing a circuit to be at special events throughout the region. He rejected the idea. He had a good location and was developing more business than he actually wanted or could handle without hiring some help.

You see, Obie Taylor started building his food wagon after his seventieth birthday. He was on social security, and could almost survive on that. He had a good pickup truck with a camper shell on it. He had a very comfortable house trailer. Everything he owned was completely paid for. He had the good sense to see he'd acquired enough wealth. To get more would mean longer hours, more pressure, hiring more helpers, keeping more books, filling out more paperwork.

Obie was happy to be a small hot dog king on a busy small town street. He might or might not decide to start making hamburgers. He was satisfied to do as he was doing as long as his health remained good. He had good enough help to allow him to get away for a few days for some gold panning in an area only sixty or so miles away, something he enjoyed doing. He knew most of his customers by first names, and enjoyed selling good food at low prices.

Obie was wealthier than many folks with more money!

The fact is, Obie could easily have made ten times as much, or more, by gearing up for special events throughout the region. He could have made another food wagon or two, to place at different places right there in his small town, and hired good workers to operate them. He had come into a small amount of sudden wealth. He was wise enough to realize that was enough.

Mr. Kroc developed the McDonalds franchise chain with a similar idea. He took that similar idea far beyond a small food wagon parked near a street junction. Fast food at low prices. People do like to eat! They often return for more, if they get a good deal, are well treated, and they like the fare. Something does not have to be an entirely new idea to succeed. It can be a somewhat different or somewhat better way of doing ordinary sorts of things. Such as serving up something to eat.

SERENDIPITY

According to Webster's II desk dictionary, serendipity is a noun that means the faculty of discovering desirable or valuable things accidentally or unexpectedly. Serendipity is a fine word to add to the vocabulary of anyone seeking sudden wealth. That group of people puts themselves into paths where encountering desirable or valuable things accidentally or unexpectedly is more common than uncommon. It becomes not at all accidental, and not too surprising when great discoveries happen.

Is it luck? To some degree. It's more putting one's self in the path of the right sorts of things to happen. It is vision, persistence, and, yes, a bit of good luck.

BUYING GOLD, SILVER, JEWELRY, AND COINS

There's many coin shops around the country, especially in cities and larger towns. There are few to none elsewhere. There are many coin collectors, a few avid ones, a host of incidental, casual collectors. Few persons in that group are extremely knowledgeable, but most of them know more about the subject than does the general populace. Only a few have attained a fairly total grasp of the subject. Those are the best dealers and the most avid collectors. The total number of all these collectors, wise and otherwise, is but a tiny percentage of the entire population. It is not within this more knowledgeable group where Eben Fine does his buying of gold, silver, jewelry, and coins.

Eben Fine is not this man's real name. His story could only be told here under an understandable cloak of anonymity. He frankly did not want to be bothered by people reading about his successes and plaguing him to tell them in endless detail his hard-learned way of doing things. He is too busy to be bothered, and values his privacy too highly. There' a few others like Eben, doing more or less the same sort of thing, but nobody has ever done it better than Eben.

The man, over a number of years, developed something of a buying circuit. He goes only to small towns, to cool places in the summer, warm places in the winter. He never remains in any town longer than two days. He then heads down a predetermined road three or four hundred miles to another town.

About a week to ten days before he comes to a town to do his buying, he arrives there to insert some well thought out newspaper advertising. He uses both local newspapers and the giveaway advertising papers, putting in half to full page ads. The basic ad never changes. It lists what he will buy and the sorts of prices he will pay. The primary difference between one ad and another is usually the name of the motel where he will be staying.

Eben aims these ads at the huge mass of people entirely outside the dealer and avid collector status of the gold, silver, coin and jewelry world. He knows that many small town people have a few old coins, a broken ring or two, maybe a few various pieces of jewelry, watches, and some odds and ends with gold or silver values. He goes to small towns for the simple reason that few buyers of such items frequent those small towns. Individuals who have this type of material will often search their drawers and closets for the items, given an opportunity to sell them. The advertisements, in the local papers a week to ten days before Mr. Fine arrives, offer such an opportunity, along with enough time to get together those bits and pieces.

Eben gets a modest sort of motel room. He has found that the best motels bring lesser results. People see in finer clothes, expensive cars, and the best motels someone who surely is there to take advantage of them. Eben wears a plain suit and drives an older model, ordinary car. He could but does not wear all sorts of jewelry.

He limits his stay to two days. One day in some places is sufficient. He is available for business in his room from about ten in the morning until eight or nine in the evening.

Eben most of the time hires an off duty policeman for security reasons. He is well aware that coins and other valuables along with sufficient cash to buy such items can and often does attract the attention of would-be thieves. He also carries a hidden high caliber pistol, for which he has a permit.

His procedure is simple. He allows only one potential customer to enter the room at a time. The police officer takes care of much of that, asking people to either wait or to come back in a short time if there is another customer already in the room.

Eben's working area is only a card table and a couple of chairs when a customer enters the room. Only a small scale, a calculator, some sheets of paper, recent quote sheets on metals and coin prices, and a couple of pens and pencils are on the table. No previous purchases are in sight. There is no visible money.

After a few friendly greetings, Eben inquires if the customer has brought items for sale. He is not there for chit chat, will not carry on long conversations about coin collecting, weather, or anything else other than a possible purchase of gold, silver, jewelry, or coins. He will also look at, consider, and perhaps buy watches, diamonds, and various collectibles.

Eben Fine briefly conveys all this in a courteous, pleasant manner. He avoids slickness, glibness, or overbearing mannerisms. He does his best to keep the meeting right to the point.

He explains that he buys most gold and silver strictly by weight and the metal content of that weight. He ably shows his customers percentages based upon karats, pointing out that a ring or other object often contains less than half gold. He is not interested in numismatics. If the customer believes he has a coin of greater numismatic value, Eben encourages him to keep it. He pays a base price for certain types of coins, no more. He will offer somewhat more for obvious key coins, but it will be only a smaller portion of Red Book prices. The same with fine jewelry. He is not going to buy bracelets, pendants, or other jewelry for anything but a percentage of the current metal value.

When he gets across that point, he carefully weighs the gold items to be purchased, then the silver items. He does some figuring on the percentage value of each piece. He gives a single offer on the amount of gold, then an offer for the silver. He makes an offer on other items, such as watches or tokens. If there still is a ring, bracelet, or other items the customer held back, items he really would like to buy, he will then sometimes slightly increase his first offer if they wish to include the item or items held back.

Whatever deal is struck, Eben pays cash on the spot. He makes out a duplicate receipt, asks the customer to sign the top copy, and hands him the bottom copy after he or she signs. There is a friendly parting.

The items purchased are carefully stored away, out of sight. Any bills or change is put away. Used pieces of paper are cleared from the table.

The next customer is invited into the room. The same sort of scene follows.

Not every person who comes into Eben's room sells what they brought. Not everyone remains calm or pleasant, but Eben is sure to do so. He does his best to part quickly, on a friendly basis, with those who decide not to sell. He will not argue about prices, nor change his offers once he makes them. It is interesting that some of those who leave the first day without selling return the second day, willing to accept his offer. Eben never says a word about their leaving. He is not concerned that some people decide not to sell. He will not haggle with those who return wishing to argue over prices.

When he leaves, he usually drives on past the town where he next will stop. This is to set up the advertising in another town still farther down the way. After doing this in maybe two or three towns, he returns to the town he bypassed. He has already rented his modest room for a certain two days.

On the next year's circuit, by the way, he does not often return to the same town. He goes to a different town, perhaps fifty or a hundred miles distant one way or the other.

The reason for doing so is simple. His circuit is more than large enough to never have to return to a particular town in five, ten, or even twenty years. He knows that the bulk of those who have items they would sell very likely took advantage of the first opportunity. Those who held back may well continue to hold back. He hopes to advertise in a town where no such opportunity as he offers has come along in a long time, if ever. Simply put, he does not intend to sit idle in his motel room for two days, with few or no customers.

Eben usually has two to three customers per hour, sometimes six to ten, one right after the other, for ten or more hours per day. Thirty or more customers is normal. He often pays fifty to several hundred dollars for what each of his customers brings him. If possible, he likes to take off for a mid-afternoon lunch. He eats a good breakfast well before ten O'clock, many days that having to do him until late in the evening.

Some weeks he can visit two towns, but it averages out to about three visits in two weeks. That usually means about six different towns a month. Eben's circuit most years lasts only six to eight months.

Approximately half of the remaining

four to six months of the year is spent by Eben Fine in selling his purchases. He sells most of the junk gold and silver through the mail, along the way, carefully packaging and shipping it to dealers with whom he has done business for many years. What takes the additional time is the sale of finer items he buys along the way.

He does not buy much at numismatic prices. Nevertheless he acquires many coins of varying numismatic value. Eben Fine has as fine a grasp of coin values and coin grading as any major dealer. Better than many, for that matter. He knows when a true gem coin or finer bit of jewelry is put on the table!

He attends a few major coin shows during each year, sometimes here or there along his circuit. That is where he sells his better coins. He knows a few jewelry dealers, and visits them annually to sell the better pieces he has purchased. He knows the better buyers of tokens, watches, and other collectibles. The mail can take care of many of those kinds of things.

A strong point must be made here. A person would never know by Eben's facial expression that a high quality 1916D dime has just been thrown upon his table along with some very ordinary silver dimes. He does not twitch an eyelash if an 1877 Indian head cent is placed along with various other pennies. If an extra fine necklace is shown him, he neither encourages nor discourages acceptance of his offer. The same for extremely rare gold coins. He simply states what he will pay, and calmly accepts the customer's decision.

What sorts of prices does he pay? There are no set guidelines. It varies between thirty to fifty percent of actual value on ordinary metals and coins, even less on the finer objects.

During the remaining free months,

Eben Fine does some traveling, fishing, and yard work in his fine but modest home located in one of the more pleasant areas of this country. Only a few close friends know where he lives. It is easy to see why he likes his privacy. He is able to do what he wants to do, for long ago, Eben Fine encountered sudden wealth.

FROM WITHIN

You do not need a ready made blueprint, should you seek a path to sudden wealth. Your best waybill for such a search lies within you. Your own experiences, your own hopes, your memories, your ambitions, these portions of yourself contain the best possible means of creating a novel, original means of striving for success. You may have an unusual hobby, and expertise that could furnish others as much pleasure as it has you. You may do something unusually well, and could easily adapt that into a service or a product highly desirable to others. You may know where stockpiles of unusual raw materials exist, materials that are inexpensive or even free to you, which you know how to turn into worthwhile objects. You may know how to combine very common, ordinary items, thus creating unusual and possibly valuable results. You may know recipes, plans, methods, techniques, or systems passed down through your family that other people would find helpful or fun. Such things exist in most people, unfortunately never developed, never used.

Do not dismiss such ideas as impractical simply because it seems ordinary and commonplace to you. Many a personal idea has taken years to develop, and the developer, living every day with it, does not recognize it as the unique treasure it often truly is. Others may tell you, "You ought to do something with that idea!". Most of the time such suggestions are shrugged off, ignored.

"It's too simple," you may have said several times, if pressed too hard. "It would already have been done if it was worth doing." That just is not so. Most good ideas are simple. It only takes reaching down inside, siezing the idea, and doing with it whatever must be done to make solid reality out of merely an idea.

Look within yourself! Have you already within you a partially developed waybill to sudden wealth?

ROY SMITH, CACHE HUNTER

Treasure hunting, as far as most people are concerned, amounts to some adventurous tales in books or magazines about unusual people taking almost impossible risks trying to recover fabulous wealth. Most people find a few such stories interesting, but they really do not believe the reality of treasure. Considered not to be real, treasure hunting is for the most part ignored. A small but substantial number of folks go so far as to buy detectors. Some of this group use detectors, and a few even do rather well at it, as a hobby. A very small number out of that mass of people do extremely well.

An even smaller number of individuals ARE treasure hunters. The amazing truth is that few if any of them would fit anywhere into the popular image of what a treasure hunter is thought to be. These few true treasure hunters have chosen to go after lost and hidden caches of wealth, and have educated themselves to be able to do so. Detectors are but a tiny part of their approach. Almost universally, they are, first, good researchers, able to talk well to people, second, observant, persistent hunters well able to use detectors and a good many other tools of the trade when required to do so.

This select small group goes about its business in a quiet, unobtrusive way. They are seldom noticed in what they do. For the most part these are individuals working on their own, usually seeming to be doing something entirely different than trying to find treasure. There are some partnerships, and at times two or three will pool their talents in one effort or another, but this is not as commonplace as individuals quietly going it alone.

One of the best of them is a fellow we will call Roy Smith. He started looking for caches in the mid 1960's, mostly because he had an uncle who'd successfully hunted for caches for many years. He never became interested in coinshooting. Looking for accidentally lost coins and artifacts simply did not interest him. His uncle had come up with five or six good caches over about a twenty-five year period, so Roy knew that it could be done. The old man took him under his wing one spring, so to speak, when he saw that Roy was interested and willing to listen. Roy was about to graduate from high school at that time, and not sure where or what he really wanted to do. He did not come from a family or an area where going to college was commonplace, and most of the local available jobs held little or no interest for him. He reveled in the attention his uncle was giving him, and did his best to warrant it.

Fairly decent metal detectors were available by the mid '60s. Roy bought one and was able to convince his uncle that it was more than an interesting toy. One good but frustrating lead his uncle had worked on for many years was Roy's first project, and that inexpensive detector paid for itself a thousand times over.

It was a family story, his uncle's lead, the sort of lead that makes true cache hunters drool. An old, miserly farmer, grandfather was known to have regularly saved and buried gold and silver coins. Upon his death a good portion of the wealth the family knew him to have saved could not be found. Some was recovered, but the major portion of the old man's savings was not found.

Roy's uncle had looked for this off and on for years. He had a 50/50 split arrangement with the heirs, who still owned and worked the farm. He had ready access to the property. He had almost worn out a couple of probing rods, yet had never found a trace of the well hidden stash. The detector was something new.

The likeliest spots, according to the family, was either the old orchard or along one of three pasture fences. The old man had often disappeared into those areas when he wanted to hide money away or get money for a major purchase. The family estimated that an amount between eight to fifteen thousand dollars had been secreted by the old man. It was all in gold or silver coins, buried deep in one or more containers.

Roy's uncle had probed along the three pasture fence lines and criss-crossed the old orchard. He had inspected thickets in the same area, indeed any probable spot hidden from sight. All those hours of searching had for years been fruitless.

Roy set in with a will, using his detector in his uncle's footsteps. Along the first fence line he found two broken plows, several dozen horse shoes, and several partial rolls of old barbed wire. He stopped digging staples, short pieces of wire, nails, and other small trash, realizing that what he sought would give a larger signal.

About a third of the way down the second pasture fence, beside a double fence post, Roy got a weak but firm signal. It was not loud, but it was somehow different than the small trash. He figured that it was something deep.

He started digging, testing with his detector every so often. The signal improved as he went down. At almost three feet his shovel struck something solid. A bit more digging, widening the hole around whatever it was, he pried out a quart jar buried beneath the broken top of an old cast iron heating stove.

The jar contained both gold and silver coins. The excited boy ran to get his uncle. Once out of sight, inside the barn, they counted out a face value of $475.50. $320 of it was gold; five ten, and twenty dollar pieces.

The find was divided equally with the delighted property owners. Roy and his uncle sold their share within the following two months to a coin dealer in a nearby city for not quite $4,000. His half of that cash seemed at the time like a lot of money to Roy. It was a taste of sudden wealth.

The owners of the property were delighted to have the uncle/nephew team continue to look, working on the same split basis if more caches were to be found.

"Just go on with what you were doing, Roy," his uncle told him. "You seem to be on the right track." Following that advice, young Smith worked down that second fence line, then the third, and on into the old orchard. Within the next three weeks he and his uncle dug up four more jars very similar to the first one. Each contained both gold and silver coins. Each was buried near some unusual arrangement of fence posts, each was covered by some large piece of cast iron. Roy's uncle believed the old man had done that to avoid breaking the jars when he wanted to dig up one of them.

After this, several weeks passed with no additional recoveries. Everyone agreed that they would stop for a time. Roy and his uncle felt that they perhaps should allow themselves some time to get away from what they had been doing, some time to think about it.

Roy's uncle gave him some good, hard advice at this time.

"We'll see what you're made of now, boy," the older man told him. "You have a wad of cash money, you have coins worth even more. Now we find out if you can keep your mouth shut. Go raise a little hell, if that's what you want to do, but keep your mouth shut. You come up with finds like we've just made, you are your own worst enemy. Brag about it, talk about it, show it off, and you'll have more trouble than you know how to handle! Keep your mouth shut, keep what you are doing to yourself, and nobody will bother you when you want to go on with what you are doing."

Roy Smith did raise a little hell. He chased girls, or in all truthfulness a number of them chased him. He drank some. He came too close to making some bad friends. He made some dumb mistakes.

He did manage to keep his mouth shut, and he soon noticed that the girls and new friends stopped coming around as often when he reached the end of that first wad of money. He decided that he honestly did want to sell any of his share of his coins so they would come back for more partying.

Instead of that, he hunted up his uncle to ask if enough time had passed. Fall was coming on, and the insects and vegetation would not be as great a problem as it had been throughout the summer. His uncle had smiled a knowing sort of smile, and agreed.

Roy Smith did not know until a good many years had passed on by what a superb lesson in "common sense" his uncle had gotten through to him. That, and an overall attitude and approach to treasure hunting were two magnificent, priceless gifts from his uncle.

They broadened their search that fall, making several more recoveries. Each one was in a similar sort of jar, buried in much the same manner. Roy's uncle finally felt they had done well enough. They had only found about two thirds of what the heirs believed their grandfather had buried, but Roy agreed with his uncle that the old man must have ranged farther than anyone thought. This they kept to themselves, knowing they might wish to try again, sometime in the future.

Roy's uncle died, that winter. He had not been very well for a long time. Roy's treasure hunting career had begun with explosive success, but suddenly he found himself alone. No back-up, no more good advice, only his own sense of direction to guide him. Independence is a magnificent but demanding gift that few individuals know how to handle.

Many young fellows would have stopped right there. Roy had considerable money. Strangely enough, Roy almost felt that his uncle still was with him. The old man had never said too much, but actions do speak louder than words. Roy had for some months observed a successful cache hunter, took in the few things the old man had told him, and had tasted the sweet reality of sudden wealth.

His independent attempts at treasure hunting were not easy. Caches seldom have anything like an X over them. The best leads are often hidden in seldom divulged family heritage, and it takes some cultivated ability to ever gain such information. Even then a hunter has but begun.

Roy soon enough realized that his uncle's lead was truly exceptional. For almost two years he tried his best, and could not seem to find any lead upon which he actually considered to be worth spending much of his time. A few interesting stories soon proved to be only that, interesting stories.

He quietly sold more of his coins, now quite frugal with spending his money. The weeks and the months marched on by as he talked to all sorts of people throughout the area. Desperation could have led to haste, but Roy kept on plugging away.

Then his search for new leads began to pay off. Within a two week period he encountered three different leads from two old men. These were just items out of the past to the old men. Neither of them had ever really thought much about the information they had, neither of them had ever discussed these things with each other even though they were well acquainted with each other. Each had a bit different slant on each of the stories, and Roy benefited from those different viewpoints.

Roy listened well, and wrote down what he heard after each talk with the old fellows. He did not make wild small talk about treasure hunting, he just was a very good listener and heard out what both men had to say.

He was also able to learn of others that knew about the three different events, and learned enough to be able to search for additional information about properties from the county courthouse. More discussion with other people added to his understanding. He found several county maps helpful, and was able to get plats of properties involved in each of the three leads. He had names, dates, situations, and even certain amounts involved in each of the three leads. He soon enough found the current ownership of each of the properties, and began to work out ways of gaining access to those properties.

One property he simply rented. He moved into the old house there. He made a deal to cut some wood on a second property, agreeing to stack and burn any scrap he generated. The third property owner simply gave him permission to go hunting there whenever he wished. Roy never said what he was most interested in hunting on the property.

Few things work out even closé to what one anticipates. None of Roy's new leads turned out just as they were supposed to. Roy soon discovered that one cache had been recovered years before, by a relative of the man who'd put it down.

The second one he has not recovered to this day, even though Roy has gained an ever increasing mass of information on it.

The third lead, involving the old house Roy rented, proved to be more and more questionable as time went by. It eventually turned out to be just another good treasure story. Not 100% wrong, but not far from it. Even so, Roy retrieved a substantial oilskin-wrapped bundle of old currency out of the attic of that house. No story with it, no lead to it, he found it because he was living there and felt compelled to search the old house carefully. Further searching did not turn up more than a few incidentally lost coins.

Roy did not forget the old men who'd led him to these caches! He never told them the whole story, but each of them was given a substantial sum and some heartfelt thanks. Each of them were overjoyed, for they were both having an ever downward financial struggle to survive. Roy from that time on resolved to never forget those who helped him in his pursuits, and he has lived up to that resolution.

Smith worked on those leads for better than one year, and has never resolved the one. During that time he fairly well established the techniques he still is using. For almost thirty years, Roy Smith has come very close to researching, hunting for, and recovering one cache of hidden wealth a year. All these caches have been considerably less than $100,000 face value, but several of them have amounted to a good deal more than that in numismatic value.

Roy believes that his record is perhaps better than average. One recovery in two to three years would probably be a more precise expectation, and that only with sufficient careful, ongoing effort. In Roy's case, at least, his leads have tended to come two, three, and four within a short time. His research slows whenever he concentrates his efforts upon searching. He knows of a few other cache hunters, but he compares notes with none of them. A few of them may have done better than he has, but Roy feels certain that most of them have not. He steadfastly has heeded his uncle's sage advice concerning a closed mouth.

Roy gives great credit to his uncle getting him off on the right track. He realizes that he might never have started down his path to sudden wealth without his uncle's help.

WHY PEOPLE HIDE WEALTH

The fact that people hide away wealth is most appreciated by treasure hunters. To better seek out such hidden wealth, the seeker had best have some knowledge of WHY people hid away their wealth. Most caches of wealth were cleverly concealed by individuals who had good reasons for doing so. Understanding those motivations can be helpful in recovering a cache deliberately hidden in a manner meant to defy easy or accidental recovery.

The WHYS are many, but they narrow down into quite common general fears, hatreds, and ambitions and hopes broader than current means. The putting away of wealth becomes habitual. There often is an ongoing postponement of using a long-hoarded cache, often past any chance of personally retrieving the cache. The original purposes are often forgotten during the ongoing concealment, and habit takes over good sense. This is fine for treasure hunters, but it often did not help the person doing it very much. Goals often enough became ruthless obsessions. Trips were never taken, medical problems were never solved, new homes were never built, children, family, and friends were slighted because the stash became a growing deity that must at all costs be fed, certainly not used.

Many larger caches were made simply because an individual suddendly came into wealth in excess of what they expected or needed. Would you not like to encounter sudden wealth? Many people enjoy squirreling away this and that, and it is natural enough for someone with sudden wealth to wish to save as much of it as possible for an unknown, dreaded future time.

The reasons for a cache still being right where it was deposited are many. Few caches were put down by someone not intending to personally recover it, but death, disease, senility, war and a host of other lethal reasons can abruptly end the best of plans. Such terminations of plans meant well-hidden caches often have remained right where they were placed.

All of us must also be well aware that more wealth is being put down TODAY than it ever was in the past. Drug money, and other illicit stashes. Frightened middle-class citizens who no longer trust banks, savings and loans, the stock market, lawyers, and the monstrous, cancerous, federal bureaucracy, and just about every other failing institution, people who have plenty of justified reasons for feeling that way. Wealthy people, hoping to hide away their wealth, for the same sorts of reasons on a larger scale. They realize we need no Iraqui, Chinese, Cuban, Russian, or other wild-eyed enemies, that we have our real enemies right here with us. Poor people, with their smaller hoards, putting aside tiny sums they can ill afford to spare, confused and helpless to prepare for an ever-worsening future. All this today makes the caches of yesteryear pale by comparison.

Why were caches put aside? What makes a person put down caches of wealth of various sizes? Yesterday's reasons were as threatening and real as those facing people today. There are as many answers as there were persons doing such things, but knowing some of those reasons is of help in working towards quicker and easier recoveries.

A person must have some wealth in order to hide some wealth. It may not be great wealth, but it has to be above what it takes for an individual to barely survive. A gaunt beggar cannot hide away every dime or quarter, or starvation will soon forever end the begging for more. A frontier farmer must have a bumper crop to catch up with past debts, repair old equipment or buy new, get new stock, new seed, to establish a stronger financial foundation. It is surplus above that basic foundation which is hidden away. Many a child, filled with sweets from some unexpected windfall, slides coins into some nook or cranny, hoping for sweets in the near future. Many a pensioner tucks away coins and bills for assurance against the increasing problems of old age.

Small caches are legion. Children's handsful of coins. Old people's jealously guarded small troves. Early day workers' small stores of set-aside coins, a few held back payday to payday. Farmers' egg and butter money. Wives' flight from brutal husbands funds. Brutal husbands' philandering funds. Loot from poorly planned robberies, hastily hidden during flight. A thousand and one other such small troves.

There are fewer medium-sized caches, and those tend to be better hidden. Even so, the total unknown number is staggering. A small percentage of a given year's population numbers into many thousands of medium-sized caches. Many small caches were merely put out of sight, behind or under something. This sort of small cache, in any given year, has consistently numbered in the tens if not hundreds of thousands. Yes, kids often retrieved their few coins and bought sweets. Yes, many old people brought out their small savings, and fended off difficult and painful times. Yes, some caches have been accidentally found, and some have purposefully been recovered. Larger amounts have most often been hidden away with far more thought, with protective measures taken against fire, flood, and detection from accidental discovery.

A few years ago a Minnesota woman

found that she was dying of cancer. Hating lawyers and the taxation authorities, she swore that "the damned lawyers and the damned IRS would not get her money". She buried it, in a line of jars and cans starting at her chicken house and running up towards a windmill. An acquaintance of mine got wind of the story, thought he had a deal to recvoer the stash with the new property owner. He began the recovery, at which point the owner told him to get off his property. The man brought in a bulldozer, in rainy weather, to dig out the scattered caches more easily. Soon broken jars and torn cans were scattering muddy coins and shredded currency down the soggy hillside. Authorities heard about the mess, and the new property owner found himself in all sorts of trouble. He ended up losing more than merely the dead woman's cache. The lawyers and the taxation authorities got it all, and then some.

Such hatreds and dislikes are common reasons for hiding away one's wealth. An aging aunt or uncle may not like their nieces and nephews, and resolve that their kin will not get any of their money. That Minnesota woman, hating bureaucratic vultures, is far from being an unusual case. Our indifferent, impersonal, often arbitrary, often cruel taxation system breeds hatred, fear, and distrust. Such feelings often generate such actions as attempts to hide away hard-earned wealth.

If you are able to figure out a particular type of why certain individuals cached money, you probably will do well at recovering that type of cache. A few quiet souls for years have looked for small egg and butter caches on midwestern farmsteads. KvM estimated that there was a minimum of one such small trove in one of four farmsteads throughout our breadbasket states. He may have been a bit conservative.

The point is, specialization aids in acquiring enough knowledge and skill in a given area to more readily recognize leads and seek recoveries. Haphazard approaches simply do not often work.

Learning the whys of hiding away wealth makes a seeker of treasure into something of a detective. Observation, careful listening, and other persistent sleuthing often opens the doors to long-closed family closets. Realize that such information can be dangerous as well as lead to possible caches. Family members or entire communities often do not wish certain long-closed doors to be opened. One can often come onto a perilously thin line between discreet cache hunting and the potential of blackmail, theft and all sorts of other illicit activities. There is no sympathy here for those who would cross that thin line over into what could well be called the dark side. To locate a long-hidden cache, and recover it, is one thing. If you KNOW that wealth belongs to somebody, such recovery is something else. It is called theft. Doing that sort of thing can get one imprisoned or even killed. There are untold numbers of stashes that require no ethical bewilderment. The caches of fifty or more years ago do not carry the risks and tricky problems of today's drug, political, smuggling and other huge new stashes. Yesteryear's depositor is not waiting nearby with an automatic rifle.

Learn a few of those whys. Settle for those sorts of things you can go after nearby where you live, and do so without stepping on toes that probably will kick you to pieces. If it is only kids' caches, a few coins at a time, be comforted that there have been many, many kids for as far back into history as you want to go. If it's wives' hidden stashes, saved for whatever purposes, that makes a good bit of opportunity for you.

Keep at it. You may do so well you, too, will have a reason why to hide away your wealth.

HIDING PLACES

Every would-be treasure hunter should know as much as possible about hiding places. Confirmed treasure seekers often consider looking for hiding places a game, a challenge of wits between the hider and the seeker. Consider it a game if you wish, but always remember you have the serious goal of recovery. We must remember that things were not hidden away to be easily found by either accident or intent. The hider's concern for his cache was that it could not easily be found by anyone else. If the hider did a good job, his or her cache probably has remained exactly where it was placed if something prevented the hider's retrieval. Death, imprisonment, mental disability, flood, fire, war and many other circumstances are enough to keep the hider from retrieving the cache. It takes an astute seeker of such caches to find them.

Detectors have helped in such searches, but the best of detectors are of limited help without some understanding of how things are hidden.

The secret of hiding places is volume. It takes space to hide anything. The best place to hide something is to put it right out in the open, but disguise it in such a way that it seems to be something other than what it is. Valuable items often do not take large amounts of room. The tales of loose bricks in fireplaces, hollow spots in bannisters and columns, chambers at the ends of closets and hallways, or small vaults built into foundations are not just tales. Those hiding places, and many others, have been used over and over to keep items of value out of sight.

What all such techniques have in common is that a volume of space is made to look like something else or to be unnoticeable. The hider does not want for strangers to even guess that a particular thing actually serves as a hiding place. The base of the bird bath may be hollow. Holes large enough to hold coins may have been drilled into solid beams. Plumbing pipes may carry wealth, not water or sewage. False floors may hold down more than insulation, insulation itself has been known to contain wrapped bundles of currency. Never forget a plain old hole in the ground.

Each and every cache takes up a certain amount of room, occupies space. That which hides wealth may be no more than board width, perhaps plaster, concrete, bricks, or even wallpaper. It may be in a difficult, out of sight place. For instance, a vault could be placed beneath where a solid workbench makes seeing the wall in which it is located impossible to see. Or it could be above high shelves, well out of normal line of sight.

Such places don't even have to be fully enclosed. A friend very recently found two hundred dollar bills and a fifty tucked between two joists. A one by four tacked on the bottom of the two joists to make it look solid kept the bills from slipping to the floor. This was in a motel room, by the way, and had been put there who knows who, when or why.

You see, how clever and well engineered a hiding place is depends to a great degree on how often the hider wanted to get into it. There really are three main sorts of caches. Short term, where the hider needs to add to and take from the cache at various times. Those kinds of hiding places have to be easy and quick to get in and out of. Mid term caches, where no access is needed very often, but is necessary several times in a given year, must not demand difficult access . Long term caches, money put down for the future, these can be very hard to get into. The hider does not expect nor want to get into the hiding place soon or often.

Always realize how small a store of value can be. A roll of ten or even twenty dollar gold pieces, twenty, thirty, or even fifty of them, can fit in a very small space. Such a place can be mortared into a wall, boxed in between studs in a wall, hidden in an art object or decoration, or concealed in a thousand other equally well hidden spots. Such a cache could be in a steel pipe, that obviously should be there, many feet higher than anyone's head. It could equally be down a pipe into the ground, far out of casual reach.

If it is a cache of diamonds, or some other small but valuable items, the space can be much smaller. Currency, also, requires such a small volume good hiding places can be devised that defy detection.

Numerous caches of ordinary coins were made simply by having a slit in a wall, or into a pipe or some other kind of tubing. The slit could easily be disguised or hidden behind a picture or some other object. Wall vaults of this sort, and pipe caches have come up with surprising regularity these past few years.

Any hollow object can hold small coins, jewelry, currency or other valuables. Posts, beams, furniture, railing, shade rollers and curtain rods, and so on. Trim board has often been pried off and then put back over a tidy little recess full of cash.

We all must realize that we cannot go around prying into all likely looking hiding places. One has to have a reason to search a place that thoroughly. If one form or another of research has not led you to a certain spot, you'd best not be knocking out foundation stones and prying off loose boards. Property owners don't much care for that sort of thing, even if they have given you permission to search the premises. You had better know that there is the probability of a cache being at a given site before you begin a careful search. There is a huge difference between careful, thoughtful treasure hunting and vandalism.

Keep uppermost in mind, leave no trace of your search. If you pry off a board, carefully replace it. Reset nails. Replace stones, even mortar them back into place if what you have done leaves an obvious mess. As coinshooters try to leave no visible traces of their probing, cache hunters have even more stringent tidiness requirements.

Consider your searches a game, if you will, but keep well in mind your serious goal of recoveries of caches. That demands of you thorough research and responsible hunting techniques. You need not be a one person wrecking crew to seek and find the hiding places you hope to find.

Much of your effort must and should be looking for anything out of place, anything too obvious. Especially with short term caches, where adding to or taking from the cache forces the hider to get into the hiding place, it is very difficult not to leave traces of frequent entry. That often means loose boards, scrape marks, scratches, cracks, or visible seams of one kind or another. Such things may not be important to most people, but if you do want to find hiding places, such things should become obvious markers.

All this thought about hiding places is worth much less if you also have not spent enough time researching, and have come to specific sites because you believe there is a good chance for a cache to be there. Yes, if you use what many have called a scattergun approach, going from one similar site to another, and work very hard and long, you may indeed make a few recoveries. The better, more rewarding way usually is to do your homework first.

Maybe the real question is, are you a serious hunter, or are you making too much of a game of it. Sure, it can and should be fun, but is your primary goal to make recoveries? If so, at least the majority of the time, avoid the scattergun approach. Come prepared, with a strong idea in mind of what you seek. If you do have a strong, valid lead, then it truly can become a game of wits between the hider and yourself.

This is true because of the time factor, if nothing else. How many sites can you thoroughly search in your active life time? Do you want to pursue maybes or real possibilities? If you like the scattergun approach, blast away. You just may have more fun than results.

We all must get back to why we're all wanting to find those hiding places. We mostly want to find caches of value within the hiding places. That means we must go after the very best possibilities.

If you truly make a science of hunting out hiding places after arriving at a given site because of careful research, you will probably find caches on a rather regular basis. You will remain relatively calm, no matter how great or small the value of your recovery, for what you do is by then more vocation than avocation. That is good, because hyperactive excitement during the moments of recovery can draw unwanted attention.

That hiding place, and whatever may be within it, has not bothered anyone for a long time. If you work calmly and quietly, it will remain out of sight and mind. Make little mess in your work. Fix up whatever mess you do make. Let the hiding place remain as well hidden after you make your recovery as it was before you came. Nobody knew of it before you recovered it. Nobody need know of it after you recover it.

Great, is it not, some of us grown up folks still playing hide and seek?

MAX GIBSON

Max Gibson went as far as third grade. I don't believe he went to much school after that. He told me he had not. He came into eastern New Mexico when his folks homesteaded south of Portales. He remembers horsemen riding across those high grasslands with only the rider's upper body and the head of the horse to be seen above the grass. There was work to be done at home in that new land. A second grader could do chores, and free his folks to plow under that tall grass and get a crop in the ground. Even so, Max made a success of himself. If second and third grade arithmetic was all he had, he used it well, and though his writing was slow and a bit labored, he wrote down whatever he had to write. I often heard Lola, his wife, reading some story or news article to him. From that and other observations, I know he found reading to be slow and labored. In spite of it all, Max became a sharp, successful trader.

I knew him, even had the privilege of going on a few trips with Max during the seven years I taught school in Ft. Sumner, New Mexico. I have at times wondered how my own life would have differed had I followed the strong urge I had for a time to follow in the footsteps Max had so clearly made before me. I did not, for I had education Max lacked, and was working to get more. I was a school teacher. I was told that educated people do not quit teaching to take up buying, selling and trading.

Max was a trader, and was a good one. He owned a comfortable home in Ft. Sumner, on an irrigated acreage. He owned several rental houses, and a number of tracts of land. My wife and I rented one of Max Gibson's houses the first year

I taught school at Ft. Sumner, and that was how I met and came to know him. He found that I enjoyed going on selling trips with him, and I accepted many an invitation, whenever I could.

There was no huge secret to the success of Max Gibson. As do most successful people, Max could recognize opportunity and act upon what he saw.

Alertness and willingness to move on what he saw kept Max more than busy enough.

Max found that he could buy good but inexpensive sweet potatoes and peanuts in the Portales area, southeast of Ft. Sumner. He would trade for them, if he could, buy them if he had to. He would then take the small load on one of the various routes he had developed throughout New Mexico.

He would stop at this or that filling station. If the owner had one or a few old batteries, and perhaps a ruined radiator, Max would try to trade some yams or peanuts for them. If he could not make a trade, he would try to buy the items cheaply. When he had accumulated enough batteries or radiators he would haul a load of one or the other over to Lubbock or Amarillo.

At times he would get a load of potatoes, in Colorado, or bring watermelons or citrus out of south Texas. Or some other load, if the opportunity arose, preferably something that could be purchased reasonably in one place and sold easily at a higher price elsewhere. If he could trade, so much the better, for Max realized those items would sell or trade elsewhere.

What Max did with those loads of yams and peanuts made a big impression on me. He did not have fifty dollars tied up in a load of produce, in those late 1950's. He was selling loads of batteries for four and five hundred dollars in Lubbock and Amarillo. He was doing even better on the radiators. I clearly saw that he was making in one week as much or more than I was making, teaching school, in a month.

Max knew what he was doing. I doubt in retrospect that Max could have outlined his methods clearly, but he fully understood at some deep level exactly what he was doing. He was working for himself. He bought as low as possible, at the source, traded whenever possible, and sold at a higher price where the product was in demand. Few economics majors can do better than that.

With more education, Max probably could have done well in some larger arena, probably on Wall Street itself.

I am delighted to have gone somewhat out of my way, on one of my trips, not long before Max Gibson died, in 1985. In spite of increasing frailty, he was as sharp and ornery as ever. I do hope that somebody will remember me as fondly as I remember that marvelous trader, Max Gibson.

IF YOU DON'T KNOW, ASK AN EXPERT. REALIZE THAT HE MAY NOT KNOW THE ANSWER, EITHER.

In the pursuit of your dream you will often find a question to which you don't know the answer. Many days there will be several such questions. Some of them will be directly in your path to success, partially or entirely blocking further progress. You must have a good answer, you needed to have it last week. Do not be afraid to admit you don't know. Above all, do not hide your ignorance from yourself. Find out who most likely has the correct answer. Go to that person, and ask.

Always be aware that for some questions there may not be adequate answers. The answers may be incomplete, and they may not be correct, even when from the mouths of "experts". If your dream has taken you past the point of correct answers, and you find yourself on the cutting edge of new knowledge or a new application of old knowledge, you may be in a better position to search out the correct answers you seek than anyone else. Even so, do not hesitate to go to this or that person who may know things you do not.

If you are working with clay, for example, a life long brick maker may know immediately some properties of clay that you do not know. So might a potter, a geologist, a constructor of roads or foundations, and who knows how many other diverse specialists.How many people know that clay goes into paper, cat litter, and filler in all sorts of commodities. If you are working with clay such knowledge could possibly save you all sorts of false starts.

A lot of wheels have already been created and put into use. You don't have to reinvent the wheel.

THE TOYS OF JACOB FARLEY

Some boys remain boys even after they reach manhood. Jacob Farley says that is what happened to him, that he will probably always be only a boy at heart.

As a boy, Jacob was fascinated with toys. As he aged the fascination only deepened and matured. The play eventually became avocation, the avocation became vocation. Jacob worked as a machinist for a number of years, but that was only to make a living. Eventually he used his tooling skills to repair old toys and even create new ones.

By the time Farley was out of grade school he already had a room filled with all sorts of toys. His own, his grandparents, his siblings, his friends, and any toys thrown away by others, all sorts of toys.

By the time Richard Farley was out of high school he had begun to concentrate on mechanical sorts of toys, wooden, metal, plastic, anything that was well constructed and did something. Tractors, old banks, trucks, robots, vehicles on wheels, tracks, legs, just about anything that was somehow functional. Other toys he had accumulated rather indiscriminately before, Jacob began to trade in high school for mechanical sorts of playthings.

Many neighbors, recognizing the love of the boy for his hobby, gave him old or partly broken toys cluttering up closets and attics.

Somewhere along the line, perhaps before he even reached high school, Jacob began to realize the value of old mechanical toys in good condition.

Others would have considered it misfortune, but when a trader in those early years bought four old banks from him for what turned out to be a ridiculously low price but made young Jacob think he was getting a good deal, Farley thereby actually started along his path towards sudden wealth.

It so happened that Jacob several months after selling the four banks ran into a man who'd bought one of them from the trader. The man was an avid, knowledgeable collector, and had paid the trader more than ten times for only one of the banks than what the trader had given young Farley for all four.

Jacob Farley did not become angry, or at least not too much so. He used the incident to his own benefit. From that first collector, he began to learn of and meet other collectors. He sold another bank to his new friend, at a price he would have never believed possible only short months before. He began to discover what collectors wanted.

Jacob already by that time had some real understanding of how and where to hunt for the best old toys. He was already a good trader, and he quickly was getting better. He was old enough to enlarge his search area, going on the bus to nearby towns because he already had found and acquired most of the old toys near home.

When Jacob was in his senior year of high school, he learned of and attended a convention put on for the benefit of traders and collectors of toys. He took with him a large number of his collection. He traded some. He bought a few others. he spent most of that time selling the majority of his stock for a very substantial amount of cash. This time there was nobody able to take advantage of Jacob. He made all sorts of new contacts, and thereafter began a correspondence with several of them that was to last for years. The most important thing, the convention stimulated Jacob into greatly expanding his search area, doing more research, and his sales gave him enough money to do some strong buying of good pieces.

Yard sales, garage sales, junk and antique shops, estate sales, these were Jacob Farley's primary targets. He found many a bargain, for he seemed in most places to be all alone in his search. Many valuable toys were almost given to him. People seemed to have no idea at all of such items' value, indeed almost were anxious to get rid of them. Jacob knew the value, and learned to usually buy at the asking price without blabbing about what he knew. He soon learned when someone was asking more than they thought an item was worth, and at such times he would haggle for a far lower price.

Unlike the stamp or coin fields, there at first was no organization of buyers and collectors. Jacob had to find his own way. Prices were low, but it was hard to find enough collectors. It was Jacob's fascination with what he was doing that kept him going. His innate belief in the value of the items in which he dealt kept him on track. Admittedly, his toolmaking skills fed, clothed, and housed before he finally became highly successful.

Success seems to come more often to those who truly love what they are doing! Jacob Farley will always remain a boy, playing with toys.

NUGGET HUNTING WITH A METAL DETECTOR

Charlie Rush has been right in the middle of the new gold rush that has quietly gotten started during the late 70's and has grown ever since. Before then, ground mineralization made hunting for gold nuggets with metal detector a difficult if not nearly futile effort. Detectors responded to black sand and hot rocks on an almost continual basis, completely masking if and when a nugget was detected. A constantly sounding detector is little more useful than one that never sounds. Charlie knew all that first hand, because he tried every way he could think of to hunt nuggets with a detector long before detectors designed to do the job came out.

Charlie Rush is that quiet sort of person who doesn't do much talking. That is even more true when it comes to what he has done with nugget hunting. He quietly goes about his business, smiles when he reads or hears some of the more outlandish stories about his chosen field, and continues to successfully hunt gold nuggets. Modest in dress and demeanor, Charlie conducts himself in a way that attracts little attention. He does not wish to be noticed. He told his tale only when he knew that his real name and actual hot spots would not be divulged.

In those earlier days Charlie did a great deal of dry washing, and was fairly successful at it. He did not like the crowded placer areas along all too many streams, with novices carting in the very latest sluicing and dredging equipment. Many such people spent far more than they would ever recover in gold, were sloppy and dirty in setting up camp, all too often were lazy, drunken, and not at all the sort of people he wanted to be near.

When the very first detectors with very low frequency and a little ground balancing ability came onto the market, Charlie Rush was one of the first buyers. He knew where nuggets were probably to be found, he'd just never had anything before then that would do the job. His dry washing explorations made him believe that desert areas had never been worked as long or hard as most stream placers.

Sure enough, Charlie almost immediately began finding nuggets. He knew where to go. He had thought of the best, simplest possible ways of searching for nuggets. He was willing to work hard with equipment that at first was anything but perfect. He kept up on each and every improvement, not depending upon wild advertising, but carefully testing any new units before buying one.

His technique was about as simple as anything could ever be. He went to a good area, one known for the production of good gold nuggets, and began to hunt. When he found a nugget, he slowed down.

Charlie would set a gold pan a few feet away from where he wanted to hunt. Near that he set the small plastic bucket in which he'd been carrying the gold pan. He removed wristwatch, rings, and anything else metallic. He never wore steel toed shoes. He carried a lightweight, strong shovel in one hand, the detector in the other. He bound a strong magnet to the end of a stick, and that he hung on a hook he'd fastened for it on his belt. It rested on his hip, out of the way.

When the detector gave off a good signal, he centered the target, and dug up a partial shovel full. This he deposited into the gold pan. He then checked both the pan and the hole, knowing the signal would be one place or the other. He quickly would probe the dirt in the pan with the magnet. If the signal had been caused by a nail, bit of wire, bolt, or other iron trash, he would throw it into a sack he had for that purpose. He did not want to ever find junk a second time. Metallic trash is always commonplace in placered areas, and Charlie found his system to be quick, easy, and efficient.

If it was not iron, and he could not see a nugget, he simply dumped the material into the plastic bucket and went back to hunting. He knew that the signal could have been caused by a slug, bird shot, or a tiny piece of brass. He could find out later without using too much time there in the field. If he saw the nugget, of course he removed it from the pan, and put the nugget into a small container. He always checked the pan for another possible signal. If there was none, he did not put the dirt into the bucket. He always checked the hole for another possible target.

Charlie wanted to spend his time hunting, not taking up precious daylight with sifting around in dirt after hard to see targets. He could take care of it after he was through hunting. His shovelsful of dirt were small, because he was highly efficient at pinpointing his targets. Iron targets were quickly found and the dirt from that shovelful did not go into the bucket. In this way, he limited the amount he had to carry back to camp or vehicle.

There are many good dry placer areas throughout much of California and Arizona. That's where Charlie Rush has done most of his hunting. His working areas read like a listing of the days of '49, as far as California goes. He has done well around Quartzite, Arizona, but he now works more often in less well-known areas. Charlie has no desire to be near a hoard of mostly novice hunters.

He has spent time in Montana, summertimes, and tried a few spots in Idaho, but usually soon heads back to his old stomping grounds. Charlie made one trip to Australia, and did well there, but he believes it to be no better than several of his favorite locations here in the states.

Charlie Rush has wisely never equated far away with somehow better. He has turned down invitations to go work in Central America and Alaska. To prove his point, he almost always did much better than his friends who invited him managed to do. He never caught some strange disease, as some of his friends did. His expenses were far, far less. His life was less hectic.

Rush has about a ten year old twenty foot travel home. He pulls a four x four Toyota behind it. He maintains both vehicles extremely well, changing oil, tires, belts and so forth long before most people would think of doing so. He wants to be comfortable, and he doesn't wish to suffer needless breakdowns in the out of the way places he frequents. By having the 4 X 4 he can park the motor home in an easier spot and still be able to reach harder to get to spots. He likes to stay in an area as long as he is doing well, seeing little reason to go here and there, adding up miles instead of nuggets. He leaves if the weather gets too bad, for he has hot weather spots and cold weather spots and can hunt more or less the entire year.

Charlie does not like to get too specific about amounts of nuggets or money, or about precise locations. He nevertheless once found over 100 ounces in a single day. He has found a number of nuggets, usually in a matrix of quartz, of sixty or more ounces. On one extraordinary day he recovered 163 small nuggets. None were more than two pennyweight. He found many more of the same sort of nuggets on following days, over 700 of them before he felt he'd fairly well worked out that remarkable small area. He has yet to have a 500 ounce year, but he came close to that unfulfilled goal in three different years. Charlie dreams of a thousand ounce year, but sometimes wonders if he will ever break the 500 ounce barrier he's not yet reached.

Charlie especially likes to work the tops of hills and hillsides. Gullies and dry washes where bedrock is nearly or entirely exposed can be highly profitable. Many ravines, however, have considerable overburden atop the bedrock, making any practical search with a detector almost impossible.

When he finds an area where richer deposits have considerable depth, Charlie puts aside the detector and goes back to dry washing. Most of the time, however, Charlie Rush likes to be swinging his detector in one prime area or another.

Charlie Rush has several boxes buried deeply and well. He calls them his "social security". He eats well, takes care of himself, goes where he wishes and does what he most wants to do. That is what encountering sudden wealth can do for a person.

"Hunting for nuggets doesn't mean sudden wealth," says Charlie, "Sudden wealth comes when you find them!"

SUDDEN WEALTH FROM COMIC BOOKS

Sudden wealth can arrive in one large, unexpected windfall. It happens that way, often enough, but usually must be recognized and seized upon before the opportunity rushes on by. Not often do such strokes of good fortune return once they are ignored.

Joseph Stanski, or that's what we'll call him, came upon one such opportune situation and acted upon it. As with many windfalls, it turned out to be the first of many opportunities as good or better. He would not have had them if he had ignored that first grand opportunity.

Joseph Stanski at the time was what can best be described as a "hippie". It was the time of flower power, rebellion against the establishment, rejection of old values. Joseph had long hair, sloppy clothing, and did most of the sorts of things that lumped him and his friends together in the general "hippie" category. Few in those days would have given him any chance at all of ever doing anything but smoking some pot and contemplating his navel.

So much for generalizations, and viva la ability to recognize and seize upon opportunities.

Joseph saw an ad in a newspaper. Someone wanted to sell some old comic books. He'd always loved comics, reveled in them at the expense of school work and household chores. The ad caught his attention, and he called the telephone number given there.

What he found was beyond his wildest fantasies. It turned out that an old widow of a lifelong magazine distributor had placed the ad. The distributor had passed away. She could no longer live alone, and was trying to clean out her house and storage areas so the property could more easily be sold. She was getting ready to move into a geriatric health care center.

Her husband for years had monthly put away all the unsold comic books from his distribution area. Month after month year after year. The attic was full. Closets and storage areas were full. They had to go. No, she did not want to sell part of them, she wanted them all removed. All of them, and soon.

Joseph dickered with the old lady for a time. He had little enough money. She wanted several thousand dollars. He scarcely could come up with one thousand dollars.

She finally told him he could have them all for $1,500, but he would have to immediately clean up the attic and other storage areas. She named the items she wished to keep, said he would have to remove everything else. Joseph agreed.

Somehow he begged or borrowed from friends enough to rake up the required $1,500. For almost three days he hauled comic books and other things out of the dusty attic and storage areas, using a borrowed pickup. A friend's father reluctantly allowed him to store everything in a big shed. He had to promise to find different storage quickly.

Joseph did some quick hustling. He located several avid comic book collectors. They wanted to go through everything he had, but he asked them what they were most interested in buying. He took them only some of the ones they hoped to buy, gave no inkling of the stacks he had piled every which way in that big shed. When they bought everything he took them, and did not haggle over what he asked, he realized he had stumbled into something good. They had looked at him rather strangely when he said he wanted a dollar apiece, and promptly paid it.

From those few sales he was able to pay back the money he'd borrowed from his friends. He rented a different shed, and moved his new stock. He started sorting and categorizing. Those first sales had scarcely dented the small hill of comic books.

It was a few months down the road when he learned he'd sold one $250 first edition, and several $50 and $60 titles for a buck each. Comic books had already begun to gather importance as collectors items. He'd unknowingly also let go a good many five and ten dollar copies. Joseph may have fussed at himself somewhat, but he did not complain to the buyers. They had already been coming back, wanting more, even at much higher prices.

Within those few months he located and rented a small store front. There was enough storage there, so he had to once more move his stock. He built shelves as cheaply as possible, and began displaying comic books.

Many readers would recognize the name he chose to call his new establishment, those who have discovered that old kids' comic books are now collector items with real potential for increased values over the years. Joseph, although what he did was not all that different from a few others in the same business, would rather keep a low profile. He has learned many tricks of the trade since that first stroke of good fortune, and talks little of it to strangers. Competition has become fiercer in the field, and there are no longer as many attics crammed full of old comic books as there used to be.

Comic books are serious business to Joseph Stanski, fun but not funny. The door to that attic was Joseph Stanski's entrance to sudden wealth. From that fast start he within a few years had three comic book stores and two warehouses. Much of each year he was out looking for more accumulations and going to comic book trade shows.

LOST LEDGES OF THE WEST

Sudden wealth comes in many forms. Is there a treasure hunter alive who'd not like to come upon an exposed vein of rich ore, with visible beads and stringers of gold laced through it, or wide planchets of native silver? How about a ledge of ore so rich in gold the beads and globules of amber material seem to cascade in a melted butter manner down through the surrounding rock? Or crystalline formations of the yellow metal, brightly casting back any ray of light, wires, filaments, and filigree of marvelous natural artistry?

There's many a tale of lost ledges. A few such tales have a verifiable basis of facts. Many less verifiable stories enter the nebulous realm of legend and fantasy. Valid, verifiable tales are what honest to goodness seekers of treasure want to hear about. Such people leave fabulous legendary stories to prospectors of the armchair variety.

Simply because a ledge was discovered, then lost, does not mean that it does not exist. That many an extraordinary outcropping was discovered, lost, and never rediscovered should neither be surprising nor too hard to believe. Most such discoveries were made in rough country, under adverse conditions, often about as difficult to reach these days as they were back whenever. Many veins and ledges are not large, are difficult to pick out in the rocks about them, and are often covered by rockslides, vegetation, or soil. Many are in areas where the summers are insufferably hot, others are where winter comes and stays for half the year. High elevations, steep slopes, insecure footing, harsh weather conditions, and a host of other detriments make many areas tough places to search.

Such lost ledges do exist. A few such tales have led to rediscovery, at which point the lost ledge soon enough became a working mine. Many others have never been rediscovered. Those await someone persistent enough to seek them, as do other ledges never before found. Remember a few years ago, when a teenager recognized a profitable ledge of gold ore not far out of Idaho Springs, Colorado? Miners had walked across it for years on their way to less profitable spots.

The good tales are not just legends and wishful thinking. In 1906 a Swede brought seventy pounds of superb ore down off the mountain into Ouray, found alongside the trail from Lake City. He had taken refuge in some overhanging rocks during a sudden blizzard. While waiting for the storm to let up he noticed a thin ledge of what he knew to be extremely rich ore. The seventy pounds brought him $7,300, a big pile of cash in those days!

A man named Daniely, while driving a water tunnel near National, Nevada, encountered a true mother lode. The men hid their fantastic discovery, hoping to return to it when mining operations there shut down. None of them lived long enough for that dream to come true. A couple of friends tried to get at it, they also failed. It's still there.

There's a ledge, still open to the sky, near Mud Lake, Idaho. All sorts of people have looked for it, it was even seen accidentally two or three times by those not looking for it, who could not find it again when they found out just what they had seen.

North of Yuma, not too far from the Colorado River, a ledge of rotten yellow quartz, full of gold, may still be hidden beside a palo verde tree. Not much of a clue, for that is a land where grow many palo verde trees, but there are other clues.

All the western states have many such tales. Montana, Utah, Idaho, California. Colorado, with its high mountains seeming to tumble one against the other, boasts many a good story long hidden by jumbled slopes a deep winter snows. Many have read of the lost Buck Rogers vein, near Eagle. Finding Eagle is easy enough, thereafter it swiftly becomes less easy. New Mexico, Nevada, Oregon, Arizona, Wyoming, every western state has its share of such good stories. Be careful, they have even more tales that are far less valid. Going into rough lands in pursuit of less than possible stories is not too bright, and can prove to be lethally dangerous. Thirst in a hot land can quickly kill the unwary. Freezing weather has terminated many a poor unprepared person. The law of gravity has no mercy, and treading a rockfall or cliff edge risks breaking that inflexible law and one's bones along with it. Searching for lost ledges is not for the unwary and ill-prepared!

If one would seek lost ledges with any real expectation of finding one, knowledge is the key. USGS, BLM, state and county and other maps are of vital help. Every scrap of knowledge of the story is required, knowledge of the area's terrain, climate, and other critical factors is necessary. An understanding of the fundamental geology concerning gold and silver ores is a must. A lost ledge seeker had best know what gold or silver ore looks like. Without this sort of comprehension the seeker is apt to find more wild geese than lost ledges.

A helpful book dealing with this subject in detail is LOST LEDGES OF THE WEST, by this author. It is a 96 page compilation of over thirty tales of lost ledges. These were carefully selected as being some of the most valid and interesting such stories. This $9.95 edition is being made available to readers of this book by merely mentioning their reading this book. Send request and $8.00, to LOST LEDGES, Drawer 71, Deming, NM 88031. The book will be sent postpaid. The book cannot assure your finding a million dollar pocket of high grade gold ore, but it's fascinating reading and gives some helpful, down to earth advice.

One needs a starting place with hunting for lost ledges. One at a time, come to think about it, that's enough. A person does not need to find more than one of this sort of thing. The Swede's seventy pounds of ore, worth $7,300 in 1906, would be worth at least twenty times as much today. Would you haul seventy pounds upon your back down the mountainside for $146,000 or more? That is true sudden wealth! Many such early finds of ore were valued at $10,000, $30,000, or even more than $100,000 per ton at $17 an ounce or less.

That means one important thing. A ledge does not need to be huge, a mere pocket of such material can be worth fortunes. Such pockets can contain hundreds or even many thousands of ounces of gold, all in a volume not as large as most kids' closets. It does beat dirty tennis shoes and rumpled shirts, does it not?

The big problem associated with lost vein structures, is that small volumes lost in vast areas, often concealed by brush, rocks and all sorts of rough terrain, are not easily found. Hunting a lost ledge is rather an ultimate challenge, a most difficult quest. The potential rewards are great, but the difficulties seem to be almost overwhelming. Again, knowledge can help even up those horrid odds. By learning as much as possible, rediscovery of the most frustratingly lost ledges moves into the realm of being possible.

Even hostile environments become less severe when one learns when and how to enter them. Brazenly hot deserts in July are often somewhat temperate during February. Six foot deep January snowdrifts are gone by August, often replaced by banks of colorful wildflowers waving gracefully in warm breezes. Modern plastic water containers hold more than old canteens, and four wheeled drive vehicles can carry far more than the old prospector's jackass. Equipment undreamed of in earlier days is available to today's would be lost ledge hunter. Maps, geologic information, and all sorts of communicative aids can help plan careful, systematic ventures. It may somehow seem less romantic, perhaps not as adventuresome, but would not the best of those old prospectors have traded in their mules, beans and bacon, rusty gold pan, and banged up tools, if given the chance, for what we have to use these days?

Why would you care to leave the comforts of home and go looking for lost ledges?

The thoughts of visible gold don't move you? You are not intrigued by sometime encountering masses of wire gold binding together chunks of rosy quartz, rich lumps worth thousands of dollars per pound? You'd not like to suddenly discover, after long and diligent search, a thin ledge of material at first glance not all that different from the surrounding matrix, that upon closer inspection shows amber bits and globules gleaming through and through that ongoing material, dipping to what unknown depths into the earth? You'd not like to pick up such specimens, at that moment realizing that you hold many ounces of gold in your hand, that hundreds of equal or greater specimens rest there before you?

If not, have you considered specializing in doing crossword puzzles?

ANONYMOUS

The anonymity of the individuals within this book is quickly obvious. Undoubtedly most readers would prefer to know the real names, the exact locations, the detailed, pinpointed realities. This book, however, is not meant to be an expose'. The individual stories here are written with the understanding that the tales could be told in a confidential manner. These are real people. Names in the book are not real, for the individuals here prefer not to be highly publicized.

Many readers would undoubtedly like to talk to the unique persons inhabiting these pages. There are all sorts of unanswered questions they would like to ask.

That is exactly what these individuals do not want. They do not care to be questioned about what they do. They'd rather be left alone to do what they do. Their privacy, their anonymity is precious and vital to them.

Their stories could be told, but only if important details were kept totally confidential.

Put yourself in their places. Would you like to be interrupted by total strangers in your pursuit of what you are about? Someone you do not know, unexpectedly at your door, someone you've never heard of on the telephone, strangers asking all sorts of detailed questions about what you do and how you do it?

No, none of us need this sort of distraction. Therefore the anonymity of these special individuals is honored. They are not sports stars, actors, or musical idols who need and seek publicity. Nevertheless, hopefully the tales in themselves will be interesting and helpful enough. No expose', here, no blueprint for anyone to copy, but perhaps encouragement for those who would do similar things to look more deeply within themselves.

Should you ever discover your own path to sudden wealth, you will surely equally wish to remain anonymous!

JOSE SILVA

Jose Silva got his financial start in Santa Fe, New Mexico. He came from Mexico in his early twenties, had little education, but saw a wide world of opportunities when he first arrived in Santa Fe. Pushcarts are common in Mexico. It was natural for Jose to acquire a pushcart and attempt to make a living in a way he understood. His English was poor, at first. That limited his job opportunities. He saw that it was possible to work for himself, however. Jose was from an agricultural area in Mexico, and did not want to merely change locations of field work, even if from grinding poverty to the somewhat higher wages paid in the U. S. He would rather take vegetable products others had grown, fill his push cart, and sell them.

His first efforts were centered on buying green chiles, trucked up from the Rio Grande river valley around Hatch. Most of his first customers were of Mexican heritage. Jose was unaware that chiles and other Mexican foods were a rapidly growing market product throughout the United Sates. He just knew the chiles sold well. His lack of English with plenty of Spanish speaking customers wanting more and more chiles eased his simple entrepreneurial start. A corner where he could place his cart once located, he was in business.

It did not take Jose long to realize that fresh green chiles are at best a seasonal product. He could extend the season somewhat by selling ristras, those beautiful hanging clusters of red chiles, or bagged dried chiles, but there was a cruel time limit no matter how innovative Jose tried to be.

To make matters worse, it gets cold in Santa Fe during the long, hard winters, making dealing from a pushcart a harsh test of endurance. There were fewer and fewer customers to buy fewer chiles of any kind.

When Jose was invited to go with an uncle to Yuma, to bring back a pickup load of oranges and grapefruit, he leaped at the opportunity. He could at least for a time get warm. The pickup was almost as old as his uncle. The trip to Yuma was an adventure in itself. Jose changed tires, patched tires, walked for gasoline when they ran out several times, and learned a good more than he at that time knew about old carburetors, old spark plugs, and leaky radiators.

Even so, Jose and his uncle finally made it to Yuma. His uncle was not feeling well, and decided to stay for a time with a sister, one of Jose's aunts. He told Jose he just was not up to making the hard trip back to Santa Fe, not for a time. If Jose would go, there were orders from friends and relatives for citrus. His uncle would buy the load, and he and Jose would split any profits.

The citrus crop was large and the fruit was extra good that year. That had already brought down prices around Yuma. Jose was able to load more citrus than should have been on the poor old pickup.

The trip south from Santa Fe was bad enough, but the return journey was worse. Fortunately the weather remained mild, if somewhat cool, or the return trip would have become a nightmare. Jose gritted his teeth, and did what he had to do to get back to Santa Fe as soon as possible.

Once there, Jose soon took care of the orders from friends and relatives. The pickup still contained a large amount of both grapefruit and oranges. Jose did not know it, but he would never have to use his pushcart again. He took the load of citrus down to where he always set his pushcart. He set the prices higher than what his uncle had charged friends and family, knowing he could come down if he had to. To his amazement, he did not have one orange, not one grapefruit by the end of the second day there at his corner.

Pleased but puzzled, Jose went to several grocery stores. Citrus in every store was marked anywhere from a quarter to sixty cents higher a pound than his prices. The quality of the fruit was not as good. Of course people had bought and bought until he had no more to sell. They recognized a real bargain when they saw one. Jose had in two days had mastered a simple lesson in economics.

Jose Silva, you see, did not fret over what he had lost. He recognized what he had gained. He knew that his uncle would be surprised and pleased with his half of the profits, that he was expecting to receive far less. As for himself, even though the trip had been hard, he cleared several times more than he had made with his pushcart in the previous two months. It was not a huge sum, but to Jose Silva it indeed was sudden wealth!

Liking the results, but not liking the thought of another trip in that worn out old pickup, Jose spent some money on good used tires, a rebuilt carburetor, a repaired radiator many times better than what was there, and a second-hand gasoline can. He did not want to take any more long hikes after gasoline out in the middle of nowhere. He also bought a few hand tools he wished he'd had on that agonizing first trip.

All this was done in an additional two days. The next morning he was headed back to Yuma. Bad weather caught him, making up for sparing him the first trip. He soon discovered the poor old pickup also needed to have its heater repaired, and that there were no windshield wipers.

That, icy roads, near zero visibility, and strong winds, made him stop in Socorro for the better part of two days.

It was not an easy winter, but it was profitable for Jose. His uncle, after a second trip, sold the pickup to Jose. With it the young fellow made several more trips that winter back and forth between Santa Fe and Yuma. He raised his prices somewhat in Santa Fe, but kept them well below what the stores were getting for poorer quality fruit. He learned to bargain harder for his purchases, and he picked up some tangelos and tangerines when he could. His old customers were glad to see him, each time he returned. Word of mouth brought many new customers. A day or two each time back in Santa Fe, he was again headed south.

As spring came, and the citrus crop neared its end, Jose tried a load of early cantaloupes. That load proved to be marginal, and if Jose had not had a number of established customers he would have lost money.

Somehow, feeling a bit at loose ends at the time, Jose happened to run into a fellow who'd been gearing up to sell planting stock. Tomatoes, peppers, cabbage, and some petunias. The man's mother had just passed away, in a different state, and he wanted to go back and settle up her estate. Someone had suggested that Jose might buy the plants, if the price was not too high.

Jose knew little of such things. He feared that a cold snap could freeze the plants. He wondered if he could sell that many plants, keep them watered enough until they sold, and if he really wanted to find out the answers to all those hard questions.

The man had not found another buyer, however, and made him such a low price on the lot Jose decided to try it.

Nice, warming spring weather blessed

Santa Fe that weekend, and Jose sold all his young plants even faster than he had that first load of citrus. This time he knew what prices the few stores offering young plants were asking. Jose asked much less, but that was still far more than he had paid. By Monday morning he was wishing that he had another such load for the following weekend.

Jose proved to be one of those rare individuals who is able to learn from what seems to be setbacks instead of sitting around moping about them. He was unable that year to find additional plants to sell. The few available to him were priced too high and of very poor quality.

Too early for chiles, the citrus season over, Jose looked around for other food products. Onions were coming into season, in the south part of the state, and he also found out about the yams and peanuts in eastern New Mexico that served my friend, Max Gibson so well. Jose was willing to risk another attempt at a load of melons, but somehow he thought it wiser to try out the onions and then a load of yams and peanuts.

His next two loads proved his judgement to be sound. He made some good money.

No path is easy, and without rough places. Jose Silva had setbacks, and he made some mistakes along the way. The good thing is, he learned from those mistakes. He found out about the potatoes grown in the San Luis Valley. He arranged with several people to grow young plants for him in the spring. He discovered that good pinto beans were always in demand, and that a choice of kidney beans, butter beans, and other types of beans were appreciated by his ever growing number of repeat customers.

Jose liked to talk with people, and many who bought from him came back time after time because of his open, friendly ways. He learned where to go to get the best crops in season. He sold the old pickup and got a better, larger one. He found that he did best at flea markets, and when he finally realized that not everywhere had such long, cold winters as Santa Fe, he moved to a smaller community farther south.

Jose could no doubt have started a successful produce market, somewhere, but he prefered to keep his system small enough to where he could handle it mostly by himself. He left the growing of things to others, and he made it part of his program to know who had the best products for the lowest prices. He arranged his pickup in a manner that attracted people, and his salesmanship was something to behold. There was always a good choice of the best products available, at prices lower than similar, lower quality items in the stores.

Wealth came suddenly to Jose Silva, when a small amount of wealth seemed like a lot to him. It has not left him over the years, but increased, because he stuck with a winning way of doing things once he developed it. Capable of change, as needed, but sticking with the basics.

No need to say, "Buen suerte, Jose," for he has made his own good luck!

ALFRED LASSITER, CREVICE HUNTER

Alfred Lassiter was 46 years old before he discovered the practicality of hunting for crevice gold. He'd done some dredging with friends, but did not pursue it. Alfred did not like getting wet and staying that way for hours. He could not seem to master scuba techniques, he admitedly was afraid of being under water. Nevertheless, some of what he had learned with his gold dredging friends helped his crevicing after he learned that many placer deposits are to be found out and away from stream beds and running water.

During the summer, not long after Alred's forty-sixth birthday, he accompanied Jay Williams, an old friend he'd known for several years up a side draw coming into a well-known California river frequented by many gold dredgers. Alfred had been along that river with his friends a number of times before. He never before had bothered to explore that sort of side canyon.

The old man took him to a narrow bench, well above the floor of the draw. Part of this bench was exposed bedrock and nowhere was there much overburden. The bench ran for perhaps thirty feet above the draw, pinched out by a cliff upstream, cut away by erosion down stream.

Jay had given Alfred a three foot steel pry bar and a bucket to carry. Jay had carried a sack lunch and a canteen. In the bucket was a much smaller, sharp steel bar, a small gold pan , a stiff bristled wisk broom and a soft bristled paint brush, some tweazers, three spoons, small, smaller, and smallest, a few small plastic bags, and a garden trowel. Jay told Alfred they would not need a shovel, at least not that day.

Thus began Alfred Lassiter's education into crevice hunting for gold. That day was to be the major turning point in his life. Although he did not realize it at the time, as is usually the case, he took the first step upon his path to sudden wealth.

Unloading, Jay carefully showed Alfred, in minute detail, why he brought Lassiter to this particular bench.

At some time in a dim geologic past the stream had flowed across this particular bench. The rock was granitic, crossed in several places by quartz seams. These quartz seams were usually lower than the surface of the granitic bedrock. Along many places, the quartz seams were almost hidden by an almost cement-like deposition of gravel. Over the millenia the stream had cut down to a deeper level, leaving that bench, once the bottom of a stream bed, high on the canyon wall of the wash.

Jay sat beside a quartz vein perhaps three inches wide but over two feet in length. He asked Alfred to bring him the tools.

With the small steel bar he began prying loose the gravel cemented in the quartz seam. As he removed the loosened rocks, he asked Alfred to brush off into the gold pan any loose material clinging to them. He was to then throw the rocks off to one side. Now and then Jay would use the larger spoon to remove finer material from his tiny working area, that also going into the gold pan. He had Alfred brush off the bigger rocks in the spoonful into the gold pan, and throw aside the rocks.

It took Jay about twenty minutes to thus dig down to where the quartz clearly showed for six to eight inches along the seam. He and Alfred had removed almost every rock in that space.

Jay then took the wisk broom and

with the help of a spoon removed as much of the finer materials as possible. After that was done to his satisfaction he repeated the process with the fine bristled paint brush. All this fine material went into the gold pan, which was not even a fourth full when at last Jay seemed to be satisfied.

"Let's go down and pan this." said Jay. "Then we'll come back up and eat some lunch."

Alfred was amazed at what the small pan produced in fine gold. There were a few fine flakes, but after careful panning most of the long, yellow string was made up of powdery, almost microscopic particles of gold dust.

"That's amazing!" Lassiter excitedly told Jay.

"Not really," said Jay with no big enthusiasm. "It just showed me what I thought, that we're in a good spot. Now let me show you why we came here."

Alfred looked at Jay, looked at the string of fine gold in the pan, an amount most dredgers would have considered pretty good results for several hours of work, then looked back at Jay.

The old man smiled, just a bit. "Let's go eat some lunch. Then I'll show you why I brought you here."

After taking plenty of time, eating, the old man proceeded to do just what he said. With the small pick, he began gouging into tiny cracks in the quartz. At times, after gaining some room in a crevice, he would use the larger bar and attempt to pry out chunks of the quartz.

"We could use a sledge hammer and some chisels, if we'd brought them, but I can give you enough ideas with what we have," Jay told him. Patiently he continued to pry at tiny fissures Alfred had not noticed, earlier. At times he would use the brush, one or another of the spoons, and put a bit of loose material into the gold pan.

Alfred Lassiter began to notice how the various quartz veins ran here and there across the ledge. The old man noted his observations, and agreed that a dozen other spots would have been as good a place to start as where he was. Some of the veins obviously were covered by thin overburden.

Jay continued to work for perhaps an hour. The gold pan was somewhat more than half full, for although not as much had been removed from the short length of vein, Alfred had not been throwing out any of the rocks. Jay was putting everying he took from the crevice into the gold pan.

Brushing delicately at where he'd been probing, the old man put one last minute amount of material into the gold pan.

Jay talked about the geologic situation in this spot, and described others, as they returned to the stream and carefully panned the results of his efforts.

This time there were a good many small nuggets, a great deal of coarser flakes, and a much larger amount of flour gold. Alfred knew there had to be the better part of an ounce of gold in the bottom of the pan.

"I'm ready to go home," Jay told him, recognizing the fact that Alfred would like to stay. "I'm tired, son. You come back here, if you want. I'll tell you some other likely places, too, if you want to talk, one day soon."

That night, after taking Jay Williams home, Alfred could hardly go to sleep for thinking out questions to ask the old man. There must be a thousand places Jay Williams could describe to him. What an eye-opening day it had been!

The following morning, Lassiter was told that old Jay Williams had suffered a stroke later that night. He was almost totally paralyzed, could not talk, and the doctor did not expect him to live.

Jay Williams did indeed weaken, and died three months later. He was a tough old man, or he'd not have lasted that long. Alfred never got to talk to him again, let alone have the detailed conversations he'd hoped to have.

Somehow, Alfred Lassiter knew that the part of a day spent with Jay Williams was enough of a start. Alfred hoped the old man knew how much he appreciated that precious gift of time and talent.

Alfred did more than return only to the high bench Jay showed him. He did that, of course, thoroughly cleaning each crevice there over the next year or so. He also scouted for and found several other similar spots in the same area. For perhaps two and a half years none of them proved to be as good as that first location, but were well worth working.

As does any hunter of placer gold, Alfred soon enough realized that there are really only four principal types of placer gold deposits. Residual, eluvial, bench, and stream deposits, and that is about it. As Alfred already had decided that he was not too interested in stream deposits because of the methods of going after them, that left the other three. He actually concentrated on bench placers, although it took him a good long time to put a name to what he was doing.

Residual placers are formed by the erosion of a vein. The decomposition of the vein releases the gold it carries, some of it held in the alluvial material on a slope below the location of the rotting vein. This is the sort of situation sought by pocket hunters. They will work the residual placer, but are most interested in digging down along the decomposed vein itself, searching for rich pockets at points where the vein constricts or narrows.

Over the years, in his efforts, Alfred discovered and worked a few such deposits, but that was never his main interest. He could never forget the high, dry crevices in remnants of old stream beds old Jay showed him.

Nor did Alfred ever do much with eluvial placers. Eluvial placers are those that are formed at points down a slope below their point of origin, but before erosion carries that gold into a stream.

Alfred in fact concentrated most of his efforts over the years in finding and working crevices, not the sands and gravels of bench placers. It was inevitable that he did some dry washing, for he at times came across some very good spots. As most benches are well above running water, working such placers means using some form or other dry washing technique.

Lassiter worked the crevices, and soon enough took most of his recovered material home. Often only bucketsful, then often enough drums carried in the back of his pickup. He gradually set up a small plant in a large back shed, and quickly obtained quicker, more effective ways of separating the gold from his recovered material.

He tried various pieces of equipment to get richer concentrates, from simple screens and grizzlies, different gold wheels, up to some jigs and other separators. He learned to use a vibrating table, working with an old one for a time, then discovering a plastic-topped unit highly effective with the rich free gold concentrates he produced so regularly.

He learned not to try to get out all the finer materials by mechanical and gravitational means. He learned the latest techniques of amalgamation, and made that his final clean-up step. Yes, he knew that values remained, but Alred has an ever-growing pile of tails he is willing to let some future gold seeker tackle.

Alfred Lassiter became a crevice hunter. He soon enough found other types of crevices than quartz veins in granite, such as the ones Jay had showed him. He grew especially fond of areas composed of slate-phylite. This rock formation has a tendency to break along its cleavage lines into "sheets". When such sheet-like formations are crossed by running water at any angle, portions of the sheets are broken off. This leaves very jagged, protruding pieces, with inset areas between, along the cleavage lines. This leaves many crevices, often deep and extensive, some of the best gold traps imaginable.

Alfred also hunts for old boulders once in the base of ancient streambeds, these also often hiding good amounts of placer gold.

Water no longer flows over what is left of the streams Alfred Lassiter works. He needs no boots or wet suit to work out the cracks and crevices of those long gone watercourses. That is the way he likes it. High and dry, his path to sudden wealth.

AL MCGOWEN, THE EXTRACTION OF FREE GOLD

Al McGowen was a milling man most of his adult life. It was not until he retired from extracting other peoples' minerals that he took up his attempt to extract free gold from sands and gravels. He had long seen the opportunities. It's just very tough to work full time and still follow a dream.

The ideas were well in place by the time he retired, at age 65. He had known for years many of the hard rock and placer miners throughout the Rocky Mountain west. His milling jobs gave him first hand, practical knowledge of how material matrixes flow, how particles of various weights can best be separated from each other, and how concentrates of one thing or another can best be obtained.

Al felt that huge amounts of placer gold were going through sand and gravel operations directly into concrete. He felt that much of that precious by-product could be saved without causing a single bottleneck in a sand and gravel operation. He set about to prove his point.

Al McGowen did most of his work along the Front Range, working with sand and gravel plants on the St. Vrain River near Longmont, on Boulder Creek east of Boulder, and on the South Platte River to the north and west of Denver. He is gone, now, but his son and grandson still are using his techniques, which for that matter are being used more and more worldwide. His ideas are simple and practical, and usually can prove quite effective on any stream coming out of gold producing areas.

Al worked in areas short distances from the canyon mouths along the Front

Range in Colorado. This meant that any gold in the sands and gravels was very fine, usually no larger than ten mesh and going down to about 400 mesh. That is ten openings to a square inch down to four hundred openings per square inch. Somewhat larger flakes were sometimes recovered, but it was mainly very small particles, all within a matrix of sand fine enough to pass through a 3/8 inch screen. All larger gravels and rocks were sidetracked in the classification process.

Al McGowen was fond of saying, "There can be no concentration without classification!" He did not need to work with the gravel and rocks, he KNEW through careful testing that the gold was contained within the 3/8th inch sands.

Al's collection system was simple enough. He fashioned a rag plant over which all the sands passed. The larger sand and gravel operations often had 200 tons going over a given point per hour. Small the gold particles might be, but they add up.

A rag plant is a steel launder, or sluice box. It is a large, flat-bottomed sluice, set at a proper angle to allow water to carry off the sand yet allowing particles of gold to drop out. A 200 ton per hour operation requires a rag plant fifty feet long, eight feet wide, and ten inches deep. Even smaller plants need about thirty feet of sluice, or gold will be lost.

Al kept foremost in his mind the fact that sand and gravel operations make their money by selling sand and gravel. The rag plant cannot be a bottleneck in the operation, or not even slow anything down. This often meant that the pitch and water flow in the sluice was not optimum for gold production. He often had to work under less than perfect conditions.

He tried many things, but settled upon short fibered indoor-outdoor carpeting on the floor of the rag plant, held down by offset square-holed steel punchplate riffling.

The carpet is long lasting and resilient, not crushed, torn, or matted as badly as other materials. The fibers catch and hold the tiny particles of gold as they settle through the holes in the punch plate.

Al put together a system based entirely on the simplest methods of mechanical separation. The magic of it was that he worked at it until he found what worked. There will be no effort to repeat his process here. For the reader who would like to read in minute detail the steps he took to remove gold from sands and gravels, THE EXTRACTION OF FREE GOLD, by Al McGowen is a wealth of information.

Success is a remarkable thing. I stood for many an hour by Al's vibrating table and watched a thin but steady stream of flour gold caught upon the upper riffle, slowly moving off the end into a catch basin. Negligible, that small band of gold when one looked upon the mass of sand from whence the concentrate came.

Every step so simple, but the whole of it an impressive technique for taking large amounts of gold from long untapped sources. Accomplished at a time when most men have slowed down. Done in spite of skeptical sand and gravel operators tired of hearing schemes and plans for taking that trickle of gold that usually did nothing but slow or stop the real work of the plant, the production of sands and gravels. No magic, just the studied application of simple mechanical separation techniques.

A thin trail of gold, that is a path to sudden wealth many people would like to find!

DOUGLAS RYKER, BEACHCOMBER

When most people think of beachcombers a mental image arises of some derelict, half drunken lout shuffling along the beach hoping to find enough decent trash washed up along the high tide line to keep him in alcohol for another day and night. With this picture in mind, most people do not even see Douglas Ryker. Pure and simple, Douglas Ryker is a beachcomber, as good a beachcomber as you probably could ever know. Beachcombing is not a hobby with this man, for he has found in that pursuit as sharply defined a path to sudden and ongoing wealth as there is.

Beachcombing is not an easily defined pursuit. There ARE derelicts along the beaches, wasting the days of their lives. Some beachcombers go after the larger materials drifted ashore, and never bother with sifters, detectors, or other means of recovering coins and jewelry. Some are solely detectorists, pursuing a splendid avocation, a few of whom are remarkably successful. There are a few who've made a lifelong pursuit of using simple sifting units, preferring them to detectors, and doing so with an astonishing success.

Douglas Ryker has done it all. He has the best available detectors, and uses them with amazing effectiveness. He has studied wave interactions and sand depositions. He knows most of what there is to know about tides. He has two sifters, one for wet sand, one for dry, and his whipcord toughness shows how far he's pulled one or the other of them over the years. At times he hauls load after load of driftwood and other storm beached materials off the beaches. Ryker takes it as it comes, knows the best times to do various things, and has made of his favorite beaches a highly productive domain.

Ryker advises would-be beach sifters to buy a copy of Warren Merkitch's BEACHCOMBER'S HANDBOOK. It was published by KvM of Exanimo, and remains the premier publication for anyone wanting to master the various forms of beachcombing. That is especially true of using a simple sifter. Douglas Ryker had been doing this sort of thing for a number of years before this little book was first published, but he admits he learned much from it. The instructions in it for building a simple, effective sifter are most helpful.

Douglas Ryker uses a sifter because he firmly believes it retrieves three to four times more jewelry than by only relying on a detector. He frankly is on the beaches after good jewelry. Coins are fine, but the jewelry is where the real profit he seeks exists. For that reason he has determined where the richer beach areas are. He wants to hunt where wealthy people play, and is perfectly willing to leave areas used by minimum wage and welfare recipients to others. He considers his pinpointing of the better areas, all he can really work on a regular annual basis, the basic foundation of his successful beachcombing. Simply put, one $500 ring and a $2,000 gold bracelet add up to baskets full of inexpensive silver and 10K gold rings.

Douglas has developed his own way of using a sifter. He seldom works the dry sand, except for a few choice sites often replenished on wealthier beaches. He has made himself known to and appreciated by the caretakers, and thereby has access to areas off limits to most others. Ryker does most of his sifting from just out from the line of lowest tides up to at or near the high tide mark. He likes to pull the sifter toward the beach, not away from it. He feels that the inrushing water cleans out the sands better, that way, from his sifter.

He does his best to overlap his inward sweeps, but does not worry whether or not he may have missed an inch or two. He often drives a stick into the sand, as a marker for his beginning point, but is able to estimate rather well for a good many sweeps thereafter. If he loses track, he moves the stick to a new starting point. Pulling a sifter is hard work and he does not feel that too much overlapping makes good sense.

He likes to work at night, as much as possible. He never works when the beach is full of people. He loves bad weather, for that reason. He can dress as warmly as need be for colder temperatures and nastier weather, when nobody in their right minds are out in such miserable places. His starting times are based on low tide marks. He likes to begin not long before the tides reach their lowest mark, then work as long thereafter as he feels at peak performance. Sifting is hard work. Douglas long ago found that trying to stay at it too long could lead to total exhaustion.

Ryker makes it a point to know the best points to hunt. He knows the most popular places at beaches frequented by wealthier people, often traveling to various spots during times of peak usage just to observe. He wants to know the areas of heaviest concentrations, the major game areas, where there are more sunbathers more often.

In the case of older beaches, often not used as much as they once were, or used by a different class of people, he relies on research and talking with older people in the area. He works certain spots at times, not because of what is going on there now, but because of what went on there years before.

Douglas wears a wetsuit when he works in the water, sifting or detecting.

Much of his work is done at night and in not too pleasant weather. Hypothermia is a very real danger to the unwary! He always wears shoes, for better footing and to prevent cutting or bruising his feet. He always carries a strong bag into which he puts his good recoveries. When he is detecting he also carries a meshed wire basket fitted to his waist, into which he puts all trash.

Ryker always puts the trash he picks up either into a nearby waste container or into a pile far up on the beach. The caretakers know and appreciate this, and that alone gives Douglas an open door often closed to others.

When detecting, Douglas works parallel to the beach, searching for particular zones. Long ago he realized that quarters tend to be deposited by wave and sand action and interaction in a rather narrow band paralleling the high tide line. Dimes are in a different line. Gold rings are usually in a still different band. He does not know the physics of this observation, but he considers it to be a fact and knows how best to use that observation.

Once he finds the first gold ring, and with it a fishing weight or two, he tries to visualize a band of similar objects. He does not worry about quarters, dimes, or anything else if he indeed finds such a band, knowing full well the next change of weather and tide will usually destroy the pattern he is following. He has often found ten or more rings in a short time, this way, and no few times well over one hundred.

He relishes stormy weather. Storm action along beaches often moves huge volumes of sand, sometimes gouging wide, deep cuts into what had been deep sand. This action at times exposes layers of old coins, jewelry, and fishing weights. This material has often been under deep sand for many years, and at times there is more than any stranger to such things would ever believe.

When this sort of thing happens, Douglas Ryker will work almost non-stop for as long as he can, knowing the first change in weather can move all that volume of sand back into the cuts. He tries to take advantage of these bonanza situations. More people in the past few years have learned of this sort of thing, but he has a few favorite spots not open to just anybody. He knows of a few sites he keeps an eye on, awaiting just the right kind of bad weather to create that kind of opportunity. When it happens, he moves at once.

Douglas does not try to work more than a fraction of the beaches around the country. He concentrates on a small fraction of better sites, once in a while venturing into a possibly good site new to him, but mostly now content to work the places he has come to know well. It is not hard to see why he would rather not list his favorite spots.

Douglas Ryker could take it easy, now, for he long ago found his sudden wealth. He has invested much of it wisely, kept some of his very best finds as sort of an insurance policy, and is happy to keep right on doing what he has learned so well to do. A bit less of it, no doubt, and a lot slower, but Ryker feels that his real wealth is being able to keep right on doing what he most loves to do.

FINDING THE RIGHT PATH

The idea of a person following a path from whatever starting point to some greatly desired goal makes a vivid picture. Many a good book uses this symbolism in its core plot, and such symbolism indeed can often sum up many real life situations. I admit to having used this symbolism throughout this book and hope it has seemed neither awkward nor trite. Real life plots are usually much better than fictional ones, and most of those who inhabit these pages truly chose wise paths and did not stray far from their chosen ways.

There are many paths. Some are easy and well traveled, others are difficult and are seldom traveled. Many, often those most crowded ways, don't seem to come from any special place and lead to all sorts of places you scarcely want to go.

Which path do you wish to take? Only you should determine that, and you may find that path only after long thought and search. Take too much advice from others, afraid of making your own choice, and you likely will find yourself well down some route you'd rather not be traveling. Even should you find a path of your own chosing, it probably will often become obscure. If you are not very careful you could wander off into some undesired byway. Know where you want to go, for that desire will be the best map to guide you through many tangled ways. Carry that map somewhere between your heart and mind, for you need both to lead you well.

Many are those who will stand along

the way and tell you that your path is hard and ill-chosen. They often will be right about the difficulty, for most paths become rocky, twisted, and lead to high, lonely places where only the most determined can find the way. Heed warnings of real danger, but lingering in the level, easy places will not bring you closer to your goal. Only following your chosen trail can do that.

Whatever you desire in life, be it wealth, tranquility, achievement in skills, learning, invention, or whatever it is you truly want, can be best found somewhere along a trail you carefully choose to follow.

Have a good journey!